# Quizzing Canada
## by Sandra Martin

Toronto and Oxford
Dundurn Press
1987

JW FC61 M37 1987b

Design and Production: Andy Tong
Printing and Binding: Hignell Printing Ltd., Winnipeg, Manitoba, Canada


The publisher wishes to acknowledge the generous assistance and ongoing support of **The Canada Council, The Book Publishing Industry Development Programme** of the **Department of Communications** and **The Ontario Arts Council.**

Care has been taken to trace the ownership of copyright material used in the text (including the illustrations). The author and publisher welcome any information enabling them to rectify any reference or credit in subsequent editions.

*J. Kirk Howard, Publisher*

**Cataloguing in Publication**


Martin, Sandra,
 Quizzing Canada

ISBN 1-55002-023-4

1. Canada - Miscellanea. 2. Holidays - Canada - Miscellanea. I. Title.

FC61.M37 1987     971'.002     C87-094966-7
F1008.3.M37 1987

**Dundurn Press Limited**
1558 Queen Street East
Toronto, Canada
M4L 1E8

**Dundurn Distribution Limited**
Athol Brose, School Hill,
Wargrave, Reading England
RG10 8DY

# CONTENTS

## The Questions

## The Answers

# DEDICATION

to Jeffrey and Louisa, who always ask the right questions

# Introduction

There's a story dating back to the 18th century about a certain James Daly, manager of a Dublin theatre. It seems that Daly, deep into his cups one evening, boldly declared he could invent a new word and overnight make it part of the language. His cronies sneered and, in time-honoured tradition, wagers were laid for and against Daly's claim. But Daly was a canny Dubliner; he went out and hired as many street urchins, beggars, and ne'er-do-wells as he could find, and sent them off with orders to mark the new word on every hoarding and wall in the city. The word was *quiz* and by noon the next day everyone was asking what it meant. The act of asking soon became the meaning of the word.

Whatever the words's origins — etymologists aren't certain whether to believe Daly's story, or whether it's a corruption of the Latin *quid est* (what is it?) or even a derivation from In*quis* ition or In*quis* itor (courtesy of the judicial tortures of 15th Century Catholic Spain) — we all know what quiz means now.

A Christmas or Holiday Quiz is an established journalistic tradition in many parts of the world, especially in Britain. Usually the quiz appears between Christmas and New Year's, intended as a diversion on one of those long afternoons when, sated with food and drink, drained of good cheer, already bored by Christmas novelties and gifts, one looks for something to do that requires neither conversation nor physical exercise.

Suffused with this spirit, in the past, I have concocted a number of quizzes with my husband Roger Hall to commemorate special occasions such as Christmas, Labour Day, and Canada Day for a number of journals but, particularly, the *Globe and Mail* . These exercises were, I am happy to say, surprisingly well-received, and that response has spurred me to foist on an unsuspecting public the following collection of quizzes.

What follows are ten quizzes, broadly related to statutory and non-statutory holidays in Canada. The purpose is to provide, on those days, or any day you want, a little *divertimento* from the day's "official" activities. As with all quizzes I've compiled in the past, the core of the questions relates to Canadian events and circumstances, but the nuances stretch beyond the borders of the true north. Do have fun with them.

Like all manuscripts this one was the product of more than one set of hands. I am grateful to editors known and unknown at the *Globe and Mail* and other publications, particularly to David Cobb who suggested the first one, and to Ed O'Dacre who commissioned several more. Similarly, my thanks go to Kirk Howard of Dundurn Press, but most of all to my husband, Roger, who is responsible in one form or another for much of the material herein.

Sandra Martin
Toronto
Michaelmas, 1987

# NEW YEAR'S DAY

Different cultures celebrate the New Year at different times. The Chinese New Year, governed by the cycle of the moon, is moveable and can occur any time between January 20 and February 19. Rosh Hashanah, the Jewish New Year, varies in timing as well, coming in either September or October. There are, of course, many cultural variations in the festivities, but for most cultures the New Year is basically a happy and joyous holiday with some sober reflections thrown in on celebrations passed.

New Year's Day has long been observed in Canada. In New France, and in present-day Quebec, *le jour de l'an* is a great family festival, and New Year's eve is a particularly exuberant and enthusiastic affair marked by parties at which mountains of food and gallons of drink are consumed. A highlight, in the past, was a levee held by the governor, a tradition that has been passed on to English-speaking provinces as well.

Scottish immigrants are probably responsible for transplanting a lot of the enthusiasm for New Year's because the holiday is a much more significant day in Scotland than, say, Christmas. One particular Scottish element which has been widely adopted throughout North America is the singing of "Auld Lang Syne" at midnight.

# I. FIRST THINGS LAST

1. January, the first month in our calendar, comes from Janus, the two-faced Roman God. What is the connection?

2. Certain Russian Orthodox groups don't follow the Gregorian calendar, which sets the New Year on January 1. Instead they use the older Julian one. When would they celebrate New Year's eve?

3. More than 125 countries hold a public holiday on New Year's Day. For some it is also a national day, honouring their independence. Unscramble the names of the three countries given here for whom January 1 is also Independence Day.

a. Onoremac
b. Iitha
c. Udnas

4. Which English Monarch first declared that January 1 would be the officia date for New Year's Day?

- [ ] a. William the Conqueror
- [ ] b. George II
- [ ] c. Victoria

5. Ancient civilizations sensibly equated the beginning of the year with significant seasonal events such as the equinox or solstice. What event determined the New Year in Ancient Egypt?

6. Which country calls it's New Year "Tet"?

7. January 1 has been the occasion for many other noteworthy events. Which of the following did NOT occur on New Year's Day?

- [ ] a. Lincoln's Emancipation Proclamation (1863)
- [ ] b. Commonwealth of Australia formed (1901)
- [ ] c. Union of Soviet Socialist Republics proclaimed (1923)
- [ ] d. The chimes of Big Ben in London were first broadcast (1923)

8. Of course, the day is, traditionally, an occasion for making resolutions and launching new projects. Which famous English diarist began writing on this day in 1660?

9. Complete the following sentence.

"On January 1 (a) _____, the bearded revolutionary (b)_____ _____ over-
threw the corrupt government of (c)_____ _____ in (d)_____."

10. The following prominent figures either were born OR died on January 1.
Match the names with the appropriate dates.

1.   Maria Edgeworth. novelist, born         ☐ a. 1895

2.   Sir Edward Lutyens, architect, died     ☐ b. 1735

3.   J. Edgar Hoover, FBI founder, born      ☐ c. 1767

4.   Paul Revere, American patriot, born     ☐ d. 1879

5.   E.M. Forster, novelist, born            ☐ e. 1944

## II. NEW YEAR'S DAY IN THE TRUE NORTH

Fill in the blanks to complete these historical statements.

1. On January 1, 1776, American troops under Robert Montgomery and
Benedict Arnold unsuccessfully attacked the Canadian city _____

2. The La Vérendrye brothers became the first whites to view the R____
M_____ on January 1, 1743.

3. The Canadian Citizenship Act took effect on January 1, _____.

4. The capital city _____ was incorporated on January 1, 1855.

5. British Columbia dropped the British habit of driving on the left-hand
side of the road on January 1, _____.

## III. CANADIAN FIRSTS

The first day of the year seems an appropriate time to reflect on "firsts" of
all varieties. Uncover the following Canadian "firsts".

1. When was the first census taken in confederated Canada?

☐ a.   1867    ☐ b.   1871    ☐ c.   1881

2. When and where did Canada's first railway operate?

☐ a.   Nova Scotia, 1826          ☐ b.   Quebec, 1836

☐ c.   Prince Edward Island, 1849

3. When was the first regular postal service established in Canada?

☐ a.   1608     ☐ b.   1734     ☐ c.   1867

4. When was Canada's first postal stamp issued?

☐ a.   1840     ☐ b.   1849     ☐ c.   1851

5. What was the first newspaper published in Canada?

☐ a.   *The Montreal Gazette*          ☐ b.   *The Halifax Gazette*

☐ c.   *The Globe,*  Toronto

6. When was the first powered heavier-than-air flight in Canada?

☐ a.   1907     ☐ b.   1909     ☐ c.   1911

7. When was the Bank of Canada established?

☐ a.   1817     ☐ b.   1871     ☐ c.   1935

8. When was decimal coinage introduced into Canada?

☐ a.   1858     ☐ b.   1899     ☐ c.   1914

9. Who was the first Canadian to win an Olympic Gold Medal?

☐ a.   Ned Hanlan     ☐ b.   Tom Longboat

☐ c.   George Orton

10. Where in Canada were the first Empire/Commonwealth games held?

☐ a.   Toronto     ☐ b.   Montreal          ☐ c.   Hamilton

# IV. WOMEN FIRST AND FOREMOST

Match these "firsts" of Canadian women with both the appropriate achievement and date.

| | | |
|---|---|---|
| 1. Marilyn Bell | ❑ A. Won *Prix Goncourt* | ❑ i.1982 |
| 2. Antonine Maillet | ❑ B. 1st woman cabinet minister | ❑ ii.1769 |
| 3. Ellen Fairclough | ❑ C. elected to House of Commons | ❑ iii.1957 |
| 4. Agnes MacPhail | ❑ D. swum Lake Ontario | ❑ iv.1982 |
| 5. Mary Pickford | ❑ E. won an Oscar | ❑ v.1986 |
| 6. Bertha Wilson | ❑ F. 1st .Supreme Court of Canada Judge | ❑ vi.1954 |
| 7. Sharon Wood | ❑ G. conquered Mount Everest | ❑ vii.1929 |
| 8. Marguerite Bourgeois | ❑ H. wrote first Canadian novel | ❑ viii.1974 |
| 9. Pauline McGibbon | ❑ I. 1st. Lieutenant-Governor | ❑ ix.1921 |
| 10. Frances Brooke | ❑ became a Saint | ❑ x.1979 |

# V. BEGINNING WITH A BANG

Some celebrate the passage of the new year with fireworks. Stretching that association more than a little, this question links "firsts" in the sense of achievements with the inventor of dynamite, Swedish scientist Alfred Nobel. Match the picture to the scrambled last name of the Nobel winner to the prize category and finally to the date. All are Canadians.

A

INNGATB          Chemistry          1957

NOSEARP — Medicine — 1971

B

ZEEGBRRH — Chemistry — 1986

C

NAYLOPI — Peace — 1923

D

# VI. BEGINNING WITH A BANG (PART II)

In the summer of 1987, a young Toronto athlete, was given the sobriquet "world's fastest man". Who was he and what was his achievement?

# All Saints Daze

**S**ince the second world war, Canada, more than ever before, has become a multi-lingual and a multi-cultural country. More than one Canadian in six, according to Statistics Canada, was born in another country. These diverse peoples have brought their folk traditions and practices with them with the result that many new festivals and celebrations — certainly non-statutory and frequently non-religious — have been incorporated into the Canadian festive calendar.

In this section newcomers are combined with the old standbys in a series of puzzles and questions about some well-established, but not necessarily statutory English and French-Canadian observances.

# I. SAINTS BE PRAISED

Match the saint's day, with the date, and then the appropriate explanation

1. St. Martin of Tours   ☐ a. October 3

2. St. Christopher   ☐ b. July 25

3. St. Thérèse   ☐ c. November 22

4. St. Crispin   ☐ d. November 11

5. St. Cecelia   ☐ e. October 25

☐ (i) patron saint of travellers

☐ (ii) patron of music and musicians and the legendary inventor of the organ

☐ (iii) leader of monasticism in France

☐ (iv) the "children's saint", she died at age 24 in 1897

☐ (v) patron saint of cobblers and shoemakers

# II. OTHER WAYS, OTHER DAYS I

Identify the celebration with the country or religion.

1. The birth of José Marti, January 28, 1853.   ☐ a. Czechoslovakia

2. St. Wenceslas Day, September 28   ☐ b. Jewish

3. Purim, February or March   ☐ c. Cuba

4. St. Casimir's Feast, March 4   ☐ d. Zoroastrian

5. Jamshed Navroz, March 21   ☐ e. Poland

# III. WHO AM I?

Identify the following patron saints.

1. The son of a Cardigan chieftain, I founded 12 monasteries, went on a pilgrimage to Jerusalem, was consecrated a bishop, and became primate of my homeland. My emblem is a dove.

2. I escaped after six years of captivity on a damp island only to be called in a dream to return to the land of my enslavement to preach the word of God. My emblems are snakes and the shamrock.

3. I am a much-venerated soldier-martyr, although many lack faith and dispute my glorious feat of slaying a dragon who was about to devour a beautiful maiden. My emblem is my flag — a red cross on a white background.

4. I was a fisherman from Galilee and the first to follow Jesus Christ. The infidel crucified me on an x-shaped cross. My emblem is a cross saltire.

# IV. OTHER WAYS, OTHER DAYS II

Match the festival with the date and then the country or region of its origins

1. Anzac Day

2. St. Francis Xavier

3. La Tire Ste. Catharine

4. La Guignolée

5. Apokreis

6. Baisakhi

7. St. Patrick's Day

8. Hana-Matsuri

9. St.Elizabeth of Hungary

10. Robbie Burns Day

☐ a.Dec. 31

☐ b.weekend before Lent

☐ c.April 13

☐ d.March 17

☐ e.April 8

☐ f.April 25

☐ g.January 25

☐ h.Nov. 25

☐ i.Nov. 17

☐ j.Dec. 3

☐ i. India

☐ ii. Japan

☐ iii.Goa

☐ iv.Germany

☐ v.Scotland

☐ vi.Ireland

☐ vii.French Canada

☐ viii.French Canada

☐ ix.Australia and N.Z.

☐ x.Greece

# V. ALL SAINTS MAZE

In the letter maze below find the names of the Patron Saints of : a. England;
b. Ireland; c. Scotland; d. Wales.

JGEOI4WOIHFDSOLIJHW4OUOQIW3U5POO4UNTOIYWLOJWL45ULQAO8U5LIULUL5ILI
IEHKDNJFMETWNBJEJILKUJOIFNRTNFKJI3WYHE4RYT2367476568709GJFNBGMNDSMOK
JOJKYPORUIEHFGNBHWJQWBHGCBVGMNGBHJLDSKLGJDFGHSFADADCXCVCXBVF
JRHRHGFGHBDJKDGBSDKJHSGFKJSHETKUJJHGFSEMJBVDXNBFSEHNAWLKGFDBD
IGNBRDSGJHFDBKHNJFDZBHMDASBMEHNWQGDHGFJYKIUOLIPOIPIOUIUYIYUIJKJ
IEJKHKJKKEJMDMFMSSMVNFJRJTIYIEJNFPATRICKVXVAFCSFDSGSAGWQGFEQBQER
WSTDYRFUYTIHJKJGFJDKJGJRFMNVNBFHGYHTYGJHNNMJM7IUJIUNMVNBVFDGRFG
CVCQWQWWEERRTYUTUIIOOPKLEKMHGJMFHGFFDCADXSZXXCVVBNMMCMCMNV
NBVXCXSDFGJHKJLOPOPIOUYTREWQASDFJHRJGFJHGJHRJHGHBEDJVGJKGTJDEJGVJH
YGKUJLKKMDHBMEHGFGEDFVCFSJNBHGLSKKJLFIKLCMFNMMLKJLKLKLKMLOPOPO
PUIKTYIGTJHGFJHMZSGJHGDJHDTFGZKDURJTGKZUJDHGTKZUDRHGTKZUDRHTOSIE
RUDTOIAEYROAIWUETOWSIURUTOIAUSEYDTLXKJCXBVZMNCVBLKZERHGROIFALS
JHDOIUTUYAW3098576W4E095682Q90835734P5096785Q0W386739W083485W043987U6W3P0
49WYTSLDKHGSLKXDRTJHLKZJDDXHGLKJSEU409658YW34PO09472Q30O915THSLIDTUE
0495RUYTHGOLIS5HFFKWHS4DKJRFHJS5LKIDHJGVKISE4HDTKIUAJH4DTLISE4HTGLO
ISEH4DTLOSHE4LOUHGDFSLIHRTELIH436BLKJZGFDOHPBLE64OLHDGFLIKHSE54LOIJ
HFDZHILKJYSRELIKJHDFOIU5ANDREW9P84W630P98TREU09PO4W63HPOIUJZGDROIU5
SYE6D79UW643PU9SREGDHOIL4SE509P57UQ3209857W094678W0943A760954ES709JATA9O
W54709TYZHLFOHJPSOI9EHRLZOIHJ6LOWIZHDNGVLOI5HETZSLIKFHGOP9AHVJVHH
REIGOIRETJNYTRLKTUYRJRTEKTYREKYTRKTYRKYTKTRYKKOEOOEJCDCNDSIDKKIE
RJJEJEKIDKCMNMRNMTGLHLHKEMDKFHFJDFGHJKGHJKLHJELFKIFMSDFSDDJEMX
DXX

# VI. DAILY DIVERSITY

1. Which two of the following non-loving events did NOT occur on St.
Valentine's Day, February 14?.

☐ a.    1779 Captain Cook stabbed to death by unwelcoming Hawaiian
natives.

☐ b.    Richard II of England murdered.

☐ c.    The Nazi battleship *Bismarck*  launched.

☐ d.    The Battle of Britain began

2. On November 25 we celebrate the cult of St. Catherine. Her emblem is
the wheel.  Why?

3. Where and when is Waitangi Day celebrated?

4. What special event is celebrated on February 29?

5. Which of the following events did NOT happen on April Fool's Day?

☐ a. English physician William Harvey, who discovered the circulation system, was born on this day in 1578.

☐ b. The Royal Air Force was formed in 1918.

☐ c. The Battle of Okinawa commenced in 1945.

☐ d. The United States launched Tiros I, the first weather satellite in 1960.

## VII. VEDDY ENGLISH

St. George's Day, April 23, has seen the birth or death of many famous English men and women. Identify some of them from the following descriptions.

1. The third of eight children, this son of a small-town alderman chose not to follow his father's profession and went into the theatre where he became, according to many sources, the greatest playwright of all time.

2. Considered one of the brightest flowers of a generation that was massively reduced by the first world war, this English poet died not in battle, but from a gnat bite while en route to Gallipoli; he was buried on the island of Skyros in 1915.

3. Son of a barber, and born at Covent Garden in 1775, this English painter was best known for his stunning seascapes.

4. Poet and Poet Laureate, he died in the Lake District he loved in 1850.

## VIII. HIGH AND HOLY DAYS I

Easter, the most important holy day of the Christian religion, is observed in most countries in the early spring on a Sunday between March 22 and April 25. Explain the symbolic meaning of the following

1. cross

2. lamb

3. lights

4.  eggs

5.  rabbits

# IX. HIGH AND HOLY DAYS II

Passover commemorates the flight of the Israelites from Egyptian slavery probably in the 1200's B.C.

1.  When is Passover?

2.  What does Passover mean?

3.  What is a seder?

4.  What is a Matzoh?

# X. TRICK OR TREAT

The ancient Celts began their New Year on November first, having honoured Samhain, the Lord of Death, the evening before. About 800 A.D. the Church incorporated the pagan custom by establishing All Saint's Day on November first. The mass that was said on this day was called Allhallowmas and so the evening before became known as All Hallow e'en or Halloween.

We now think of Halloween as a secular festival, a time for children to dress in costumes and go from house to house collecting candy for themselves and coins for UNICEF, The United Nations Children's Fund. Nevertheless, October 31 has seen a number of significant events throughout the years. Match the following events with the appropriate dates.

1.  birth of the Dutch artist Jan Vermeer

2.  Martin Luther nailed his 95 Theses on the Church door at Wittenberg in Germany

3.  birth of Chiang Kai-Shek

4.  Michelangelo's Sistine Chapel ceiling was unveiled

5.  death of Harry Houdini from a ruptured appendix, following a dare to a McGill University student to punch him in the stomach

☐ a. 1926    ☐ b. 1887    ☐ c. 1512    ☐ d. 1623    ☐ e. 1517

# VICTORIA DAY

The Twenty-Fourth of May
Is the Queen's Birthday;
If they don't give us a holiday
We'll all run away.

That anonymous little jingle was a schoolyard hit well before the turn-of-the-century in Canada. The period marked the apogee of British Imperialism and English-Canadians identifed enthusiastically with the vast movement that saw one-quarter of the global map painted British Imperial Red. To be a good Canadian was synonymous with being a good Briton, and the celebration of Queen Victoria's birthday was the patriotic highlight of the year. Bands marched, soldiers paraded, and politicians prattled the platitudes of the time.

The practice of observing the monarch's birthday was made an official holiday in Canada West (old Ontario) as early as the 1850s. By the 1890s a strong Imperial Federation movement had emerged and with it an enthusiasm to turn the Queen's Birthday into an occasion to salute not only the monarch but the British Empire. This Empire Day concept originated with Hamilton's Clementina Fessenden and was given publicity throughout the country by George (later Sir George) Ross, then Ontario Education minister and eventually Premier.

Empire Day was observed on the school day preceding the 24th of May holiday and formal patriotic instruction and excercises were introduced into the curriculum. Enthusiasm for Empire Day waned (as did interest in imperialism) after the bloodletting of the first world war, although there was a revival during World War II. A holiday on the twenty-fourth of May, however, remained resolutely popular and, since 1952, has been observed on the 1st Monday preceding May 25th.

Victoria Day, now largely, but not entirely stripped of its patriotic associations, is one of the major guideposts to the Canadian calendar. Exhortations are always made that no plants can go into the ground until the 24th, no cottages can be opened, no white shoes worn and so on. The following Toronto *Globe* editorial of 24 May, 1924 gives a sense of this enduring view.

*The Twenty-fourth comes just as the Canadian summer, when the weather is behaving normally, is beginning to bloom. It is the first public holiday which can be spent outdoors with comfort if the sun is shining, excepting a rare Good Friday. When the day is fine all the pent-up longing of old and young for open-air enjoyment is released and the woods, the fields, the playgrounds and the highways beckon.*

# I. CROWNED HEADS

1. Queen Victoria's birthday was the twenty-fourth of May. In what year was she born?

2. What is the birthday of Elizabeth II, our present queen?

3. Match the British or French monarch (whose realm included Canada), with his birthdate.

| 1. | Louis XIV | ☐ a. | 14 December, 1553 |
| 2. | George III | ☐ b. | 4 June, 1738 |
| 3. | Henri IV | ☐ c. | 5 September, 1638 |
| 4. | George IV | ☐ d. | 12 August, 1762 |
| 5. | William IV | ☐ e. | 21 August, 1765 |

4. What is the official surname of descendants of Queen Elizabeth II?

☐ a. Mountbatten     ☐ b. Windsor

☐ c. Mountbatten-Windsor

5. Which of the following was not a surname of a British Royal family?

☐ a. Plantagenet     ☐ b. Tudor     ☐ c. Meredith

☐ d. Hanover     ☐ e. Saxe-Cobourg and Gotha

6. Who was the last British monarch to use the name Saxe-Cobourg and Gotha?

7. What is the difference between the Heir Apparent and the Heir Presumptive?

8. Arrange the following monarchs of Great Britain in their correct chronological order.

| 1. | William I | 5. | Charles I |
| 2. | Richard I | 4. | James I |
| 3. | Edward I | 6. | George I |

9. Which of the following is **not** a residence of the present Queen?

☐ a. Buckingham Palace   ☐ b. Windsor Castle

☐ c. Balmoral Castle   ☐ d. Sandringham

☐ e. Clarence House

10. British royalty has often visited, and in the case of some notables like Victoria's father, Prince Edward, actually lived in Canada for periods of time. When, however, was the first official visit of a crowned monarch?

## II. FLAGS AND SYMBOLS

1. Identify the province or territory identified with each of the following flags.

A   B   C   D

E   F   G   H

2. Now match the motto with the correct province and translation.

I.      UT INCEPIT FIDELIS SIC PERMANET
II.     JE ME SOUVIENS
III.    MUNIT HAEC ALTERA VINCIT
IV.     SPEM REDUXIT
V.      SPLENDOR SINE OCCASU
VI.     PARVA SUB INGENTI
VII.    FORTIS ET LIBER
VIII.   QUAERITE PRIME REGNUM DEI

☐ A. Prince Edward Island   ☐ B. British Columbia

☐ C. Quebec   ☐ D. Newfoundland

☐ E. New Brunswick   ☐ F. Ontario

☐ G. Alberta   ☐ H. Nova Scotia

☐ 1. One defends and the other conquers

☐ 2.   Splendour without diminishment

☐ 3.   Seek Ye First the Kingdom of God

☐ 4.   The small under the protection of the great

☐ 5.   Loyal she began and loyal she remains

☐ 6.   I remember

☐ 7.   Hope was restored

☐ 8.   Strong and free

3. Of what is the following a description?

"Tierced in Fesse: the first and second divisions containing the quarterly coat following, namely, lst Gules, three lions passant guardant in pale Or, 2nd, a Lion rampant within a double Tressure Fleury-Counter-Fleury Gules, 3rd Azure, a Harp or stringed Argent, 4th Azure, three Fleurs-de-Lis, Or, and the third division Argent, three Maple Leaves conjoined on one Stem proper".

4. What is the description, as in question 3, called?

5. What is "castor canadensis"?

☐ a.   a type of Canadian cough medicine

☐ b.   a recent line of fishing gear made in Oshawa

☐ c.   the beaver, symbol of Canada

6. When was the present Canadian flag adopted?

7. What were some of the derisory names given to the flag when it first appeared:

a.   Pearson's pennant
b.   The Red Cabbage
c.   The Maple Leaf Rag
d.   all of the above

8. In a sense Canada had debated the need for a new national flag ever since Confederation in l867. The "great flag debate" in l964, leading to the adoption of the Maple Leaf Flag, was unparallelled, however, in terms of the rhetoric and conviction of proponents of one design or another. During that parliamentary session how many sitting days of parliament were taken up with the flag issue?

☐ a. six ☐ b. seventeen ☐ c. thirty-seven

9. A substantial number of Progressive Conservatives, under their leader, ex-Prime Minister John Diefenbaker, were particularly keen to retain the old Red Ensign design. Enough wind was generated both inside and outside the House of Commons to send endless flags flapping. The Liberals mounted an astonishing fifty speeches on the matter. How many did the Tories produce?

☐ a. 70 ☐ b. 101 ☐ c. 210

10. The official motto of Canada is *A mari usque ad mare* meaning "from sea unto sea". Where is the phrase taken from?

# III. VICE-REGAL CANADA

1. The Crown in Canada is, of course, represented by the Governor-General and the Lieutenant-Governors. Match the names of the Governors-General first with their photographs and then with their periods in office.

1.Edward Schreyer        2.Duke of Connaught
3.Duke of Devonshire     4.Vincent Massey
5.Lord Tweedsmuir        6.Jules Léger
7.Earl Grey              8.Georges Vanier
9.Viscount Alexander     10.Roland Michener

A ☐        B ☐        C ☐        D ☐        E ☐

F          G          H          I          J
☐          ☐          ☐          ☐          ☐

☐ a.1967-74   ☐ b.1911-16   ☐ c..1916-21   ☐ d.1952-59   ☐ e.1946-52

☐ f.1979-84   ☐ g.1974-79   ☐ h.1959-67   ☐ i.1904-11   ☐ j.1935-40

2.   Which pre-World War I Governor-General gave Canada a sports trophy traditionally presented in the late autumn. The sport was formerly something of a national pastime, but in recent years it has lost some of its kick.

3.   Which Governor-General was a much-decorated soldier in World War I, became a Canadian representative at the League of Nations, and Ambassador to France?

4.   Which of the following Governors-General was the son-in-law of Queen Victoria?

☐ a.   Marquess of Lorne ☐ b.   Viscount Monck

☐ c.   Earl of Dufferin

5. And which Governor-General was her son?

6. Give the name and the title of the Governor-General who was a celebrated author of adventure books (what we would now call thrillers) and provide the name of his best-known spy story.

7. Who was Canada's first native-born Governor-General?

☐ a.   Vincent Massey ☐ b.   Georges Vanier

☐ c.   Jules Leger

8. The Department of Justice decided that women might be appointed Lieutenant-Governors in 1934. In what year was the first woman appointed to that post?

☐ a.   1935 ☐ b.   1945 ☐ c.   1974.

9. Who was the first native-person to become a Lieutenant-Governor? When — and in what province?

10. In 1982 historian G.F.G. Stanley became the Lieutenant-Governor of New Brunswick. Earlier in his career he had been the person most responsible for choosing a symbol that has since become entirely identified with Canada. What was it?

## IV. THE ROYAL US AND THEM

Fill in the blanks to complete these famous royal utterances.

1. Elizabeth I. "I will make you shorter by a _____."

2. Charles II. "Let not poor _____ starve."

3. Edward VIII. "I have found it impossible . . . to discharge my duties as king . . . without the help and support of _____ _____ _____ _____.

4. Victoria. "_____ are not amused."

5. Henry II. "Who will free me from this turbulent _____"

# CANADA DAY

It was called **Dominion Day** until 1982 when our parliamentary giants in Ottawa cast aside one of our few distinctive contributions to the political lexicon and rechristened the celebration Canada Day. A prosaic and predictable title, but a holiday is still a holiday. Incidentally, the name change, which came about because of a private member's bill, passed all three stages in the House of Commons, on July 9, 1982, in a record speed of five minutes. Having thus exerted themselves, the assembled MPs decided to adjourn 55 minutes earlier than usual — in honour of the renamed holiday, of course. Later, a few conservative senators of all political stripes coughed and grumbled about the measure, but to no avail.

Whatever it is called, the July 1 holiday is a major entry in the Canadian calendar. School is out, the mercury in the thermometer is soaring, our myriad shores beckon, and if it doesn't rain (and, statistically, it usually doesn't), then all the joys of summer combine to guarantee a mellow, relaxed long weekend.

The actual date, July 1, commemorates Canada's first birthday, July 1, 1867, when the newly-minted Confederation of British North American provinces came into effect. "With the first dawn of this gladsome summer morn", trumpeted Toronto's *Globe* "we hail this birthday of a new nationality." The cheering, however, was by no means universal. As a popular movement, Confederation was confined largely to Canada West (Ontario) and the Colonial Office in London's Downing Street. Much of Quebec ignored the whole thing and many communities in the Maritimes mourned and hung out the black bunting. The potentially rich, but still largely uninhabited, western half of the country still slumbered under the aegis of the Hudson's Bay Company, and British Columbians were somewhat ambivalent about a confederated British North America. "*Plus ça change...*" a cynic might say today.

In the following Canada Day quiz, five questions are posed for each of the 13 decades of Confederation. Occasionally, the queries leave the soil of the true north — but that's a hoary Canadian tradition.

# I. 1860s

1. What was the Trent Affair?

2. Which of the following was **not** suggested as a name for the new country in 1867?

☐ a.  Tupona     ☐ b.  Efisga     ☐ c.  Vesperia

☐ d.  Mesopelagia     ☐ e.  Albertoria     ☐ f.  Cabotia

☐ g.  Cartieria

3. The effect of the Fenian Raids on both legislators and the general public is said to be one of the catalysts of Confederation. Who were the Fenians?

4. What was Louis Riel's occupation before he became a political leader in the 1860s?

5. 1867 was the year of the Canadian Confederation; it also marked the publication of a book that, it has been argued, has influenced more people than any other except the Bible. What was it and who was the author?

# II. 1870s

1. In what year were the Mounties organized?

2. Samuel Butler published *Erewhon* in 1872; everyone knows what it means backwards, but what is the full title?

3. What was the original occupation of Alexander Mackenzie, Canada's second Prime Minister?

4. Canada's first federal census was published in 1871. The total population was :

☐ a.  1.1 million     ☐ b.  3.5 million     ☐ c.  11 million

5. On August 3, 1876, in Wallis Ellis's general store in Mount Pleasant, Ontario, a young man received a telephone call from his uncle in Brantford. Who was the young man and what was the significance of the event?

# III. 1880s

1. InDecember, 1881, under the prodding of the Governor-General, the Marquis of Lorne, a Canadian institution, which would be condemned in *The Globe* as "a mutual admiration society of nincompoops" was established. What was it?

2. In 1884, 373 Canadian river and lumbermen, took part in a strange journey up the Nile as part of General Sir Garnet Wolseley's rescue column. Who was he attempting to rescue?

3. The hanging of Louis Riel engendered a nationalist fervour in Quebec which was exploited effectively by H____ M____, who became premier of that province in 1887.

4. On July 2, 1881, what American President was shot and later died? Who succeeded him?

5. 1889 saw the first performance of which Gilbert and Sullivan operetta? It was revived not long ago to bumper audiences at the Stratford Festival. And if you still haven't guessed, here's another hint: An English version of *Venezia* .

# IV. 1890s

1. Who was Canada's first native-born Prime Minister?

2. On January 24, 1897, an organization supported by Lady Aberdeen, wife of the Governor-General was launched and named in honour of Queen Victoria, who that year celebrated her diamond jubilee. What was it?

3. A test of extreme difficulty (?). Place in chronological order the following Prime Ministers:

☐ a.  Sir Charles Tupper        ☐ b.  Sir John Abbott

☐ c.  Sir John Thompson        ☐ d.  Sir Mackenzie Bowell

4. Who were Lying George Carmack, Skookum Jim and Tagish Charley?

5. What future Canadian Prime Minister was born on April 23, 1897?

# V. 1900s

1. In 1903, the Canadian town of _____, Alberta disappeared in a disastrous mud and rock slide.

2. Thomas J. Ryan of Toronto, in 1909, developed what popular indoor sport?

3. What future Prime Minister was Canada's first deputy minister of labour (appointed in 1901 at the age of 26)?

4. The following events all occurred in the same year: (a) the Alaska Boundary Treaty, (b) publication of G. E. Moore's *Principia Mathematica*, (c) the death of the painter James Whistler. Name the year.

5. What aviator became the first to fly across the English Channel in 1909?

# VI. 1910s

1. In what year was "In Flanders Fields" published by John McCrae? (What was the name of the publication in which it first appeared)?

2. How many enemy aircraft did Canadian Ace Billy Bishop receive credit for shooting down in the first world war?
☐ a.  39    ☐ b.  45    ☐ c.  72

3. Canada's greatest maritime disaster occurred in the St. Lawrence not far from Matane, Quebec, on May 29, 1914. What was it?

4. What was the name of the French munitions ship that caught fire and exploded in Halifax Harbour, on December 5, 1917 levelling a square mile and killing 2,000 people?

5. On August 15, 1914 as guns were unlimbered in Europe, what event occurred in the Americas that would greatly influence Canada's economy?

# VII. 1920s

1. Jalna was the name of the house that figured so prominently in Mazo de la Roche's 1928 novel of the same name. What was the name of the actual house on which Jalna was modelled?

2. When were the immortal lines "He shoots, he scores" first uttered by 18-year old broadcaster Foster Hewitt?

3. Two events marked a kind of Canadian Declaration of Independence from British control of external affairs in the early 1920s. What were they?

4. It was the year Valentino died; the year Winnie the Pooh was published and T. E. Lawrence's *Seven Pillars of Wisdom* first appeared. It was the year _____.

5. Canadians and Americans both cheered as radio told them that slugger _____ _____ had slammed 60 home runs.

# VIII. 1930s

1. On May 28, 1934, the Dionne quintuplets were born in Callander, Ontario. What was the name of the physician who delivered them? For a bonus point, give as many of the names of the quints as you can.

2. Who stated of the Depression, "Nobody thought about money in those days because they never saw any. You could take your girl to a supper dance at a hotel for $10, and that included the bottle and a room for you and your friends to drink it in. I'm glad I grew up then. It was a good time for everybody. People learned what it means to work."

3. What was the winning Liberal campaign slogan of 1935?

4. Match the following dates with the event or institution:

| | | | |
|---|---|---|---|
| 1. | Statute of Westminster | ☐ a. | 1938 |
| 2. | Founding of the League for Social Reconstruction | ☐ b. | 1932 |
| 3. | Oshawa Strike | ☐ c. | 1931 |
| 4. | Abdication Crisis | ☐ d. | 1937 |
| 5. | Munich | ☐ e. | 1936 |

5. What was the Regina Manifesto? As a bonus, the father of which present-day Liberal Provincial Premier signed the document?

# X. 1940s

1. What far-reaching piece of social legislation was implemented on Dominion Day, 1941?

2. Christmas Day of that same year saw the surrender of the remains of two battalions of Canadian troops and the beginnings of a long and bitter debate as to whether their sacrifice was necessary. Where were the troops engaged?

3. *Spring Thaw*, Canada's longest-running revue, had its debut on April Fool's Day, of what year?

4. Who said "Canadian women got the vote as a gift rather than as a reward."

5. By the end of the second world war, the United States had accepted more than 200,000 Jewish refugees, Britain 70,000, China 25,000, Argentina 50,000. How many had Canada taken in?

# X. 1950s

1. What is "Our Pet Juliette"'s last name?

2. On July 13, 1953, an actor playing Richard III stepped onto the parapet of a "thrust" stage in a huge canvas tent erected in Stratford, Ontario, and uttered these words "Now is the winter of our discontent/Made glorious summer by this sun of York." Who was that actor? As a bonus who was the first Canadian (and woman) to speak on the Festival stage?

3. Mix and Match:

| | |
|---|---|
| 1.Sputnik | ☐ a.1953 |
| 2.Massey Report | ☐ b.1958 |
| 3.Canada Council | ☐ c.1951 |
| 4.Cancellation of Arrow | ☐ d.1957 |
| 5.Ian Fleming's *Casino Royale* published | ☐ e.1957 |

4. What is the longest running entertainment show on Canadian television?

5. The most celebrated of Britain's "angry young men", John Osborne, had his play, *Look Back in Anger* first produced in what year?

# XI. 1960s

1. Who said "We don't intend to use Canada as a dumping ground for nuclear warheads."

2. On Dominion Day, 1962, the country's first medicare scheme came into force, and created broad and deep divisions in the medical profession. In what province did the plan first come into effect?

3. What exactly is an ookpik?

☐ a.    a Ukrainian toothpick          ☐ b.    a furry Arctic owl doll

☐ c.    a plectrum for Yukon ukuleles

4. Anne Heggtveit won the first Canadian gold medal in _____ _____ at the 1960 Winter Olympics at Squaw Valley, California.

5. What do the following abbreviations stand for:

a.    UDI
b.    5BX
c.    RIN
d.    CYC
e.    TWTWTW

# XII. 1970s

1. What did the button "Il y a du français dans l'air" signify?

2. Who was Quebec's Justice Minister during the October Crisis?

3. Match the pop hits with the year in which they reached the top of the charts:

1.    Let It Be  (Beatles)                              ☐ a.    1974

2.    Joy to the World (Three Dog Night)              ☐ b.    1973

3.    American Pie (Don McLean)                      ☐ c.    1972

4.    Tie a Yellow Ribbon (Tony Orlando & Dawn)      ☐ d.    1971

5.    Seasons in the Sun (Terry Jacks)               ☐ e.    1970

4. Which of the following is **not** a 1970s popular expression?

☐ a. Have a nice day    ☐ b. the bottom line

☐ c. getting it together    ☐ d. input

5. What was the stated cost of Montreal's Olympic Stadium before the roof was installed:

☐ a. $300 million    ☐ b. $500 million

☐ c. $700 million    ☐ d. $800 million

# XIII. 1980s

1. The rock group "The Who" had their final concert on the same night as ??? who gave his final public performance as leader of the opposition.

2. Who, and on what occasion, suggested that Joe Clark and John Crosbie see "eye to eye, cheek to cheek, toe to toe, bum to bum ... and when are those bums going to get their act together?"

3. How much money did Terry Fox's epic run across the country in 1980 raise for cancer research?

4. On September 4, 1984 Brian Mulroney and his Progressive Conservatives won the largest majority in Canada's electoral history. How many seats were won by Mulroney's party?

☐ a. 197    ☐ b. 202    ☐ c. 211

5. In 1985 three long-reigning Canadian provincial premiers retired. Can you name them?

# CIVIC HOLIDAY

**C**ivic Holiday is a happy contrivance celebrated in many parts of Canada in midsummer. It goes by several names — and by no name. In Ontario it is now generally called Simcoe Day, after the province's first Lieutenant-Governor, John Graves Simcoe. Alberta and Saskatchewan call it Heritage Day, and although popular in Manitoba and the North West Territories, neither place gives it a distinctive name. Local enthusiasm for the day evidently is not diminished by this lack of identity. In most places the date is now fixed as the first Monday in August.

This quiz will not discriminate against the unfortunates who do not — legally at any rate — celebrate Civic Holiday. After all, some recalcitrant jursidictions, like Quebec or Newfoundland, joyfully celebrate other days while the denizens of Ontario, the Maritimes and parts west dutifully toil. Quebec's unique summer holiday is St. Jean Baptiste Day while Newfoundland celebrates Discovery Day. Coincidentally, they fall on the same date — June 24.

The first Canadian holiday with a "civic" connotation occurred — where else — in Toronto in 1861. Alderman John Carr argued successfully in the City Council that September 12 of that year should be declared an official holiday "to afford citizens an opportunity for relaxation and enjoyment." Doubtless he was re-elected. The day has long since been switched to August and it has picked up a provincial connotation, but the rationale for its existence seems as relevant and sensible as ever. This quiz meanders from coast to coast and in a spurt of magnanimity reflects the interests even of those poor souls who don't have a holiday on the first Monday of August.

# I. DEFINITIONS

Select the most appropriate definition for each of the following terms.

1. Arctic Char

☐ a.  a variety of salmon found in northern waters.

☐ b.  a Baffin Island domestic

☐ c.  a green leafy vegetable found north of the 54th parallel

2. Bleu

☐ a.  a bilingual and bicultural beer

☐ b.  a Quebec conservative

☐ c.  a Québécois cigarillo

3. Tidal Bore

☐ a.  a deep cleansing laundry detergent

☐ b.  any Maritime politician

☐ c.  the high tide that enters the Bay of Fundy

4. Sourdough

☐ a.  the devalued Canadian dollar

☐ b.  a bad-tempered cook

☐ c.  a fermented bread dough used in rough baking

5. Potlatch

☐ a.  Canadian for the lid of a saucepan

☐ b.  a West Coast Indian celebration

☐ c.  a dime-bag

6. Fiddlehead

☐ a.  a book published by poet Fred Cogswell

☐ b.  an edible fern

☐ c.  a Yehudi Menuhin groupie

## 7. Screech

☐ a.  the characteristic cry of the Canadian taxpayer in the late spring

☐ b.  one-half of a Canadian comedy team

☐ c.  a dark, rough Newfoundland rum

## 8. Chinook

☐ a.  an undesireable person

☐ b.  an Eskimo toast

☐ c.  a warm wind in Western Canada

## 9. Clergy Reserves

☐ a.  an elite force of Papal troops permanently stationed in Quebec

☐ b.  sections of land set aside for the support and maintenance of the Protestant Clergy

☐ c.  a 19th century network of reservations for baptised Indians

## 10. Newfie Bullet

☐ a.  a Telefilm sponsored remake of the Steve McQueen film

☐ b.  the first shot fired in the Third Cod War

☐ c.  a derisive nickname for the old narrow-guage Newfoundland train

# II. NAME THAT PLACE

Many Canadian towns and cities were once known by different names. Match the following places with their current names.

1.  Rat Portage          ☐ a.  Winnipeg

2.  Berlin               ☐ b.  Thunder Bay

3.  Pile of Bones        ☐ c.  Vancouver

4.  Fort Garry           ☐ d.  Kenora

5.  Stadacona            ☐ e.  Cambridge

6.  Fort Rouillé         ☐ f.  Kitchener

| 7. Bytown | ☐ g. Regina |
|---|---|
| 8. Galt | ☐ h. Toronto |
| 9. Fort William | ☐ i. Ottawa |
| 10. Gastown | ☐ j. Quebec City |

# III. SCRAMBLE

Here are the names of five Canadian Prime Ministers. Unscramble them. Then take the third letter from each name to form the name of a 19th century Governor-General.

1. POOSMNTH
2. EERKABFNEID
3. NTEEBNT
4. NEDOBR
5. RLTSTUNAE

# IV. THE PEOPLES' PALACES

The following photographs are of the ten provincial parliament buildings. Can you associate the right building with the appropriate province?

A

B

C

D

E

F

G

H

I

J

# V. PROVINCIAL RIGHTS

Who made the following statements?

1. "Each little Province is a little nation by itself."

☐ a. Sir John A. Macdonald      ☐ b. George Brown

☐ c. Sir Charles Tupper

2. "It seems that the smaller the province the more trouble it will be. Columbia, Manitoba, and Prince Edward Island give me more trouble than Ontario and Quebec."

☐ a. Sir John A. Macdonald      ☐ b. Sir Wilfrid Laurier

☐ c. Alexander Mackenzie

3. "Confederation, so far, has done nothing to fuse the races, and very little even to unite the provinces . . . .From the composition of a cabinet to the composition of a rifle team, sectionalism is the rule."

☐ a. Goldwin Smith   ☐ b. John Diefenbaker   ☐ c. Sir Robert Borden

# VI. CIVIC MONUMENTS

What are the cities referred to in the following quotations? As a bonus identify the speaker or writer.

1. "This is the first time I was ever in a city where you couldn't throw a brick without breaking a church window."

2. "City of laws and saws."

3. "Into the mist my guardian prows put
   forth,
   Behind the mist my virgin ramparts
   lie,
   The warden of the Honour of the
   Sleepless and veiled am I!"

4. "I did not expect to find here in this new capital of a new country, with the boundless forest within half a mile of us on almost every side, — concentrated as it were the worst evils of our old and most artificial social system at home, with none of its agremens , and none of its  advantages."

5. "It has the individuality and the pride of a city where great things have happened, and  over which many years have passed....is as refreshing and as definite after the other cities of this continent as an immortal among a crowd of stockbrokers."

# VII. STREETSMARTS

If you were on _____Street, what town or city would you be in?
1. Danforth
2. Atwater
3. Lower Champlain Street
4. Hastings
5. Portage
6. Sparks
7. Barrington
8. Scarth
9. Jasper
10. Quadra

# VIII. THE MOSTEST

1. Name Canada's largest city.

2. What is the country's highest peak?

3. If you were in Beaver Creek, Yukon, you would be in Canada's _____ town.

4. _____ is the largest island in Canada.

5. Name Canada's longest river.


# IX. GOING TO EXTREMES

1. When and where was Canada's lowest temperature recorded?

2. The highest?

3. What is Canada's warmest city?

4. And the country's rainiest place?

5. And the foggiest (Ottawa not included)?


# X. POP CULTURE

1. Where is Canada's population most dense (again, Ottawa excluded)?

2. English and French are the official languages of Canada. What, according to the most recent census, is the next most common mother tongue?

3. What is the size of Canada's native population?
☐ a.  1, 540, 601     ☐ b.  864, 050     ☐ c.  491, 460

4. Canadian males can now expect to live 71.9 years and Canadian females 79 years. What were the comparable figures more than half a century ago in the census of 1931?

5. A century ago the Canadian population was much more rural than urban. In 1881 74.3% of the population was rural and 25.7% urban. What are the percentages now?

# XI. SIGHTSEEING

Identify the province in which the following cultural or tourist attractions are located.

1. Gros Morne National Park

2. Lucy Maud Montgomery's birthplace

3. Fortress of Louisbourg National Historic Site

4. Kings Landing Historical Settlement

5. McCord Museum

6. Elora Gorge

7. Old Fort Henry

8. Agawa Canyon

9. Folkorama

10. Batoche Battlefield

11. Dinosaur Provincial Park

12. Klondike Days

13. Cathedral Grove

14. Diamond Tooth Gertie's Gambling Casino

15. Magnetic Hill

# XII. ONE GAME AT A TIME

1. The Forum is to Montreal as the _____ is to Calgary.

2. If you received a Schenley Award, at what sport would you be proficient?

3. What significant sporting contest, staged annually in Canada since 1860, is North America's oldest annual sports event?

4. If you were given the Lady Byng Trophy, what would have been your accomplishment?

5. It's not an Olympic event yet, but according to the *Guinness Book of World Records*, a Torontonian named David Frank, on August 11-12, 1985 covered a distance of 270.483 miles in 36 hours, 43 minutes and 40 seconds. What was he doing?

# LABOUR DAY

Surely there is no better perspective from which to contemplate the working condition than a day off work. Canadians have been officially celebrating Labour Day as paid leave since the Dominion government made it a statutory federal holiday back in 1894. The roots actually go much deeper than that — and the Canadian celebration appears to have been one of those happy (and rare) occasions when we did not slavishly follow an American example.

America's celebration evidently started with the Knights of Labour, who held workingmen's parades in New York City beginning in 1882. Canada's parades and rallies to celebrate the labouring classes appear to have commenced a full ten years earlier. Some 3,000 members of 13 unions marched at Queen's Park, Toronto as early as April, 1872.

Still, it may have taken the American example to push Canadians to institutionalize the event. It was American labour leader George R. Lloyd who, in 1884, proposed the New York events should be an annual affair. His suggestion caught on and Oregon became the first state, in 1887, to make it a legal holiday although the chosen date was the first of June. Other states followed and in 1893 the occasion was fixed as the first Monday in September, that month generally being considered not only worthy, but in need of an official holiday. Canada followed suit a year later.

At that time most Canadians lived and worked on farms. Since the turn of the century, however, an industrial proletariat has developed, one that has been joined in recent decades by an immense corps of "white collar" and service industry workers. Canada is now, more than ever before, a country of employees.

It is a country too in which the labour movement has matured in difficult and occasionally contradictory ways. As with so many manufacturing and industrial companies, most of the "international" unions in Canada are merely local branches of an American parent. The establishment of a nationalist Canadian union movement has been a long cherished goal of many Canadians, and much of the history of working people in this country is the story of this struggle. In turn the political manifestations of the labour movement in Canada have reflected the fragmented ideologies of Canadian working people. What follows is intended to be a non-laborious diversion for those still struggling against the perfidious work ethic.

# I. WORKING LANGUAGE

Match the following quotations and authors:

1. "I like work; it fascinates me.
I can sit and look at it for hours.
I love to keep it by me: the idea
of getting rid of it nearly breaks
my heart."

☐ a. Thomas Carlyle

2. "The workers have nothing to lose
but their chains. They have a world
to gain. Workers of the world, unite."

☐ b. Jerome K. Jerome

3. "If any would not work, neither
should he eat."

☐ c. Benjamin King

4. "Nothing to do but work,/Nothing
to eat but food,/Nothing to wear but
clothes/To keep one from going nude."

☐ d. The Bible

5. "Work is the grand cure of all the
maladies and miseries that ever beset
mankind."

☐ e. Karl Marx

# II. UNION LABELS

Who, or what, are the following?

a. scab
b. goon
c. blackleg
d. goldbricker
e. flunky

# III. STRIKES

Match dates with strikes

1. Winnipeg General Strike    ☐ a.   1923

2. The British General Strike    ☐ b.   1926

3. The Pullman Strike    ☐ c.   1937

4. The Asbestos Strike    ☐ d.   1933

5. The Oshawa Strike    ☐ e.   1968

6. The Vancouver Sit-In    ☐ f.   1892

7. Sydney Steel Strike    ☐ g.   1949

8. Paris Students Strike    ☐ h.   1938

9. The Homestead Strike    ☐ i.   1894

10. The Stratford Strike    ☐ j.   1919

# IV. SHORTCUTS

What do the following abbreviations stand for?

1. CGT
2. AFL-CIO
3. TUC
4. CLC
5. ICFTU
6. WCL
7. WFTU
8. AUCCTU
9. ILO
10. IAMSSPRSTMSHMMTWH

# V. LEADING ROLES

Match the names and achievements:
1. Robert Owen (1771-1858)
2. Samuel Gompers (1850-1924)

3. Terence V. Powderley (1849-1924)

4. Jean Jaurès (1859-1914)

5. Louis Blanc (1811-1882)

6. Friedrich Engels (1820-1895)

7. Albert "Ginger" Goodwin (d. 1918)

8. Keir Hardie (1856-1915)

9. "King Ludd"

10. Walter Reuther (1907-1970)

☐ a. Founder of the British Labour Party; surprised House of Commons by wearing cloth cap and tweed jacket to Parliament.

☐ b. German-born Manchester textile manufacturer; avowed Communist.

☐ c. British-born American labour leader, first president of the A.F. of L. and a key figure in the move to Americanize Canadian unions.

☐ d. French socialist leader, attempted to forestall first world war by urging all workingmen to refuse to fight; assassinated for his efforts by an outraged French nationalist.

☐ e. French socialist and social theorist. Author of *L'organization du travail*, an idealistic social treatise emphasizing a theory of equal wages.

☐ f. American labour leader; tool and diemaker who came to prominence as head of the UAW.

☐ g. Mythical leader and inspiration to bands of English workingmen who rioted 1811-1816. The movement, which had no apparent political aim or cohesion, was characterized by the wrecking of industrial machinery.

☐ h. Canadian labour martyr shot by police in Comox, British Columbia, for evading the draft.

☐ i. British social reformer and socialist; pioneer of the co-operative movement.

☐ j. Influential American labour leader; Grand Master Workman of the Knights of Labour from 1876-1893

# VI. DEFINITIONS

Choose the best definition for the following terms:

1. COLA

☐ a. Company agreement to install new soft-drink machines

☐ b. Cost of Living Adjustment

☐ c. Concerted Opposition to Labour Association; a right wing political pressure group.

2. RED CIRCLE:

☐ a. A Communist trade union

☐ b. The philosophy of work to rule

☐ c. Practice of limiting wage increases to select personnel

3. MOONLIGHTING:

☐ a. An obscene gesture of solidarity

☐ b. Effects of a strike at Ontario Hydro

☐ c. Working at another job in addition to regular work

4. TIME AND MOTION STUDY:

☐ a. An analysis of the use of portable toilets on job-sites

☐ b. Physics 21 at a community college

☐ c. Work efficiency analysis

5. CASUAL WORKER:

☐ a. any government employee

☐ b. a part-time or temporary worker

☐ c. promoter of eight-day hour

6. WILDCAT STRIKES:

☐ a. Revolt and sedition at the zoo          ☐ b. Unofficial strikes

☐ c. Cultural reaction to all cartoons featuring cats by Kliban.

7. PIECE WORK

☐ a. Meeting of the Campaign for Nuclear Disarmament

☐ b. The value theory of labour

☐ c. Payment awarded according to amount of work done

8. JOURNEYMAN:

☐ a. Commercial traveller

☐ b. Qualified artisan who works for another

☐ c. Person who negotiates annual leave

9. SWEATSHOP

☐ a. Part of the Nautilus Fitness Centre empire

☐ b. A place where cooling-off periods are not mandatory

☐ c. Factory employing unskilled labour at low, low pay

10. FEATHERBEDDING

☐ a. The concern of the International Brotherhood of Amalgamated Mattress and Pillow Workers

☐ b. A necessary adjunct to any sit-down strike

☐ c. The creation of unnecessary work to earn more money

# VII.  BEAVER TALES  (I)

Link the labour leader to the union with which his/her name is associated.

1. Louis Laberge      ☐ a. CLC

2. Shirley Carr       ☐ b. QFL

3. Hal Banks          ☐ c. CUPW

4. Jean-Claude Parrot ☐ d. CAW

5. Robert White       ☐ e. SIU

# VIII. BEAVER TALES (II)

1. Name the revered nineteenth century Canadian journalist who was fervently opposed to labour unions and eventually was assasinated by a disgruntled former employee.

2. What was the highest federal unemployment rate, as a percentage, in Canadian history?

3. What was the year in which the Canadian Labour Congress was founded?

4. Who was Arthur "Slim" Evans?

5. Name another nineteenth century Canadian journalist popularly considered to be a tribune of the people, but who also was opposed to strikes.

6. Which two Canadian prime ministers first came to public notice because of their interest in labour activities?

7. What was the OBU?

8. Rank the following Canadian unions in terms of size:

☐ a.   National Union of Provincial Government Employees

☐ b.   Canadian Auto Workers

☐ c.   Canadian Union of Public Employees

9. Where, in Canada, were the first unions formed?

10. What were the terms offered by Sir John Carling to his brewery workers in the 1860s?

# IX.   BEAVER TALES  (III)

Match the following quotations with the speakers:

1. "Workers have the right to organize        ☐ a. J.S. Woodsworth
   and the right not to organize.
   Labour has the right to organize,
   but not to disorganize."

2. "Everybody wants to make money, but how many want it enough to work for it?"

☐ b. Senator David Croll

3. "My place is with the workers rather than riding with General Motors."

☐ c. Daniel J. O'Donoghue

4. "The fight is not between hand-workers and brain workers. It is not between industrial and agricultural workers. The fight is essentially between producers and the parasites."

☐ d. Roy Thomson

5. "Your excellency, I represent the rag, tag, and bobtail!"

☐ e. Maurice Duplessis

# X. POTPOURRI

1. What was the world's longest strike.?

2. Which country has the lowest unemployment rate?

3. Name an American film in which actress Sally Field plays a tough-minded, capable union organizer?

4. Who were The Wobblies?

5. What Canadian labour leader, born in Northern Ireland in 1935, recently separated the Canadian branch of the American United Auto Workers from its American parent?

# THANKSGIVING

Harvest festivals are celebrated all over the world to mark the end of the agricultural growth cycle. They are happy events that combine giving thanks for this year's harvest with performing traditional rituals to ensure bountiful crops next year. Thanksgiving remains one of the most popular of all Canadian official holidays. Unlike Christmas or Easter, its profound moral and religious connotations are largely untainted by commercialism.

Some authorities trace Canadian Thanksgiving to 1578 when Martin Frobisher gave thanks to God after being spared from a severe storm at sea in the eastern arctic. However, the more usual historical path argues that transplanted settlers from the British American colonies to the south brought the tradition with them when Halifax was established in 1749. Certainly in 1763 the citizens of that city observed a day of thanksgiving celebrating Britain's victory over France in the Seven Years War.

In the aftermath of the American Revolution, Loyalists are thought to have spread the practice of a special harvest-season day of thanksgiving throughout the area that would become Canada. They brought with them, of course, those uniquely American aspects that have marked American Thanksgiving since it was first observed in 1621 — namely, consuming roast turkey and various squashes such as the pumpkin at a family or community feast.

Official observation of Thanksgiving in Canada was sporadic until after Confederation in 1867. A dozen years later, in November, 1879 to be precise, an annual day of national thanksgiving was officially proclaimed for the new country. As in the United States, the observance was as much a civic as a religious one, since all denominations were expected to participate. Later, after the first world war, a distinctly national, and officially ecumenical spirit emerged in Canadian Thanksgivings. Dates for the observation varied, however, until 1957 when the federal government proclaimed that the date be fixed as the second Monday in October of each year. And so it has continued.

# QUESTIONS

1. Which of the following is **not** likely to be found in a traditional Thanksgiving feast?

☐ a.   roast turkey      ☐ b.   venison      ☐ c.   bear

☐ d.   pumpkin pie      ☐ e.   baron of beef

☐ f.   plum pudding      ☐ g.   cranberries

2. Canadian Thanksgiving is in October; when is American?

3. Were the celebrations ever held on the same date?

4. Match the following ancient harvest festivals with the appropriate cultures:

1.  Kern                        ☐ a.   English

2.  Sukkoth, the feast of tabernacles     ☐ b   Scottish

3   Lammas-Day                 ☐ c   Peruvian

4.  fiesta de la vendimia         ☐ d   Egyptian

5.  The Harvest Festival of Min      ☐ e   Jewish

5. What is "The Harvest Doll" (sometimes known as the "Corn Mother")?

6. After the first world war, Thanksgiving Day and _____ Day were celebrated in Canada on the same day.

7. In what is now the United States, the date most commonly given for the first Thanksgiving is 1621. Who inaugrated the event? Where? And for how long did the first celebration go on?

8. When did Thanksgiving become a national holiday in the United States?

9. In Upper Canada (now Ontario), June 18, 1816 was officially declared a day of thanksgiving. What was thanks being given for?

10. What is a sukkah? And what is its connection with the contemporary celebration of Thanksgiving in North America?

# REMEMBRANCE DAY

The war to end war ended on November 11, 1918. Ten million people had been killed in combat, twenty million more had been wounded and millions of others were dead from disease and starvation. In four years of fighting, the world and particularly Europe had been transformed: empires had collapsed, cities were in ruins, even the social order had been irretrievably changed.

The scale of the slaughter was unprecedented and the fervent hope on all sides was that no such devastation should ever happen again. Remembrance Day commemorates two things: in a narrow sense it celebrates the end of the first world war, but in a more general sense it is an occasion to reflect upon all past wars and conflicts. The day's purpose is to honour those who died and to remind successive generations of the horrors and dangers of war — in short to cool hot heads and temporize extremists.

In the United States the day is called Veterans Day, but in Britain, Canada, and places like Australia and New Zealand it is either called Armistice Day or Remembrance Day. In the United States, Veteran's Day is fixed as the fourth Monday in October, but in Canada and the rest of the Commonwealth the event is always observed on the actual anniversary of the date on which the shooting stopped in the first world war — the eleventh hour of the eleventh day of the eleventh month of 1918.

Either two or three minutes silence is observed at this hour. Wreaths are laid at local cenotaphs and many churches hold special services. Remembrance Day is a day of mixed emotions, of sorrow and hope, a day that recalls destruction and promises renewal. If there is a constant theme it is probably echoed in the wisdom of the philosopher George Santayana who wrote prophetically that "Those who do not remember the past are condemned to relive it."

The following quiz focusses, in the words of the title of a contemporary novel, on "war and remembrance."

# I. CANADA AT WAR

1. Canadians think they live in a "peaceable kingdom", but much of the country's history has been punctuated by wars and conflict. Which of the following wars did **not** involve Canada in some way?

☐ a. Queen Anne's War (1702-13)    ☐ b. King William's War (1689-97)

☐ c. The Seven Years War (1756-63)    ☐ d. King Philip's War (1675-6)

2. The Canadian colonies — French or English — frequently became ensnared in European wars and dynastic struggles, but there were also many wars or conflicts which had their origins in the new world. Match the figure with the conflict with which he or she is usually connected.

1. Sir Isaac Brock    ☐ a. NorthwestRebellion

2. Louis Riel    ☐ b. Rebellion of 1837

3. William Lyon Mackenzie    ☐ c. Seven Years War

4. Captain James Cook    ☐ d. War of 1812

5. Pierre d'Iberville    ☐ e. King William's War

3. Wars are marked by battles. Give the dates of the following battles, which either took place on Canadian soil or involved Canadian troops.

1. Lundy's Lane
☐ a. 1812    ☐ b. 1813    ☐ c. 1814

2. Batoche
☐ a. 1837    ☐ b. 1885    ☐ c. 1917

3. The Somme
☐ a. 1915    ☐ b. 1916    ☐ c. 1917

4. Plains of Abraham
☐ a. 1696    ☐ b. 1745    ☐ c. 1759

5. Dieppe
☐ a. 1940    ☐ b. 1941    ☐ c. 1942

4. What was the name of the incident during the American Civil War where Confederates used Canada as a launching pad for an assault on an American town?

5. The date November 11th represents the end of the first world war, but another famous battle took place in Canada on this date more than a century before. What was it?

## II. OTHER TIMES AND PLACES

Which one of the following events did **not** occur on November 11th.

☐ a. Ned Kelly, notorious Australian outlaw hanged in Melbourne (1880).

☐ b. U. S. General George Patton born (1885).

☐ c. Ian Smith of Rhodesia announces UDI (Unitlateral Declaration of Independence) (1970)

☐ d. The German battleship *Tirpitz* sunk (1944).

☐ e. Cease-fire in the war between Israel and Egypt (1973).

## III. OTHER TIMES AND PLACES II

1. St. Martin of Tours died on this date in the year 397. Of what is he the Patron Saint?

2. Also on this date, in 1831, an American slave who had led an armed revolt of slaves against their masters in the American south, was hanged. What was his name?

3. On November 11, 1957 _____ became the first British West Indian colony to become independent.

4. On this date in 1938 a woman named Mary Mallon died in Riverside Hospital in New York City. She was notorious — both in her native Ireland and in the United States — as an unwitting killer. What was her "crime" and by what name was she also known?

5. On this date in 1940 the British attacked and crippled the naval fleet of which Mediterranean nation?

# IV. BELLIGERENT WORDS

Identify the speaker:

1. "It would be seen by the world that Canada, a daughter of Old England, intends to stand by her in this great conflict. When the call comes our answer goes at once, and it goes in the classical language of the British Answer to the call of duty 'Ready, aye, ready'."

☐ a. Sir Robert Borden ☐ b. Sir Wilfrid Laurier

☐ c. Sir John A. Macdonald

2. " . . . well there are a lot of bleeding hearts around who just don't like to see people with helmets and guns. All I can say is, go on and bleed, but it is more important to keep law and order in the society than to be worried about weak-kneed people . . . ".

3. "I also inspected a bombed-out hospital in Luetzow Street. Several corpses were just being carried out — a touching picture. One of the nurses killed was an air-raid warden. It drives one mad to think that any old Canadian boor, who probably can't even find Europe on the globe, flies to Europe from his super-rich country which his people don't know how to exploit, and here bombards a continent with a crowded population. But let's hope we can soon deliver the proper reply."

4. "Not necessrily conscription but conscription if necessary".

☐ a. Sir Wilfrid Laurier ☐ b. William Lyon Mackenzie King

☐ c. Arthur Meighen

5. "Our best effort was on the 21st when we fought Baron von Richtohofen's 'Circus' . . . among these was the Baron whom I shot down on our side of the lines. We did not lose anyone in that fight. It is going to have a great effect on the war in the air . . . .

☐ a. Billy Bishop ☐ b. A. Roy Brown ☐ c. Raymond Collishaw

# V. MORE BELLIGERENT WORDS

Match the quotation with the author.

1. "War is much too important a matter to be left to the generals."

2. "If they want peace, nations should avoid the pinpricks that precede cannon shots."

3. "Nothing except a battle lost can be half so melancholy as a battle won."

4. "In peace, sons bury their fathers; in war, fathers bury their sons."

5. "There is many a boy here today who looks on war as all glory, but boys, it is all hell."

☐ a. Napoleon  ☐ b. William T. Sherman  ☐ c. Duke of Wellington

☐ d. Herodotus  ☐ e. Georges Clemenceau

# VI. WORDS AT WAR

Match the popular song-title with the war in which it originated, or gained popularity..

1. "Good-bye Dolly Gray"  ☐ a. The War of 1812

2. "It's a long way to Tipperary"  ☐ b. The Anglo-Boer War

3. "Tenting Tonight"  ☐ c. First world war

4. "The White Cliffs of Dover"  ☐ d. Second world war

5. "The Star-Spangled Banner"  ☐ e. U.S. Civil War

# VII. PACTS

Match the date and the alliance.

1. Dreikaiserbund  ☐ a. 1904

2. Nazi-Soviet Pact  ☐ b. 1939

3. Triple Alliance  ☐ c. 1882

4. Confederation of the Rhine  ☐ d. 1873

5. Entente Cordiale  ☐ e. 1806

# VIII. PAX

Fill in the blanks.
1. The U. S. Civil War ended on April 9, 1865 at _____ Court House in Virginia.

2. The "war-guilt" clause in the Treaty of _____ (1919) meant, some thought prophetically at the time, that it wasn't peace but only a twenty-year's truce.

3. Many military weapons are claimed to be guarantors of peace and security. One such was the Great Wall of China. A modern equivalent of that wall called the _____ Line was built between parts of France and Germany in 1929-34.

4. The Anglo-Boer war of 1899-1902 was officially terminated by the Treaty of _____ .

5. Winston Churchill: "To jaw-jaw is better than to _____ ".

# IX. WAR POETRY

Who wrote:
1. "If I should die, think only this of me:
   That there's some corner of a foreign field
   That is for ever England."

2. "Everyone suddenly burst out singing
        And I was filled with such delight
   As prisoned birds must find in freedom..."

3. "If in some smothering dreams, you too could pace
   Behind the wagon that we flung him in,
   And watch the white eyes writhing in his face,
   His hanging face, like a devil's sick of sin;
   If you could hear, at every jolt, the blood
   Come gargling from the froth-corrupted lungs,
   Bitter as the cud
   Of vile, incurable sores on innocent tongues, —
   My friend, you would not tell with such high zest
   To children ardent for some desperate glory,
   The old Lie: Dulce et decorum est
   Pro patria mori.

4. "What, then, was war? No mere discord of flags
   But an infection of the common sky
   That sagged ominously upon the earth
   Even when the season was the airiest May.
   Down pressed the sky and we, oppressed, thrust out
   Boastful tongue, clenched fist and valiant yard.
   Natural infirmities were out of mode,
   For Death was young again: patron alone
   Of healthy dying, premature, fate-spasm.

5.  "I have been young, and now am not too old;
    And I have seen the righteous forsaken,
    His health, his honour and his quality taken,
    This is not what we were formerly told.

# X. CANADA AT WAR II

1. The Canadian War Memorial at Vimy Ridge, known properly as the Vimy Memorial, sits atop the ridge of the same name, on 250 acres deeded by the French government in perpetuity to Canada. Who was the sculptor of this massive work and when was it completed?

2. Why is Vimy Ridge such an appropriate place for the monument?

3. What is a distinctive feature of the 12,000 ton base of the monument

4. What would become a significant ongoing monument to the Canadian particpation in the war was established with the formation of the Canadian War Memorials Fund in 1915, an initative which eventually permitted 116 artists to devote their time to recording their interpretations of the war. Which Canadian figure, resident in England, was behind the plan?

5. Another enduring memory of the war came through a short poem published in December, 1915 in the English magazine  Punch . It was written by a serving Canadian medical officer who died in 1918. Name the poem and its author.

# XI. THE PRICE OF WAR

The price of war is always the same: death, destruction and human misery. Twentieth-century wars — total industrial wars involving entire societies — have been more destructive in every way than those of any other period. Remarkably in a century of statistical thoroughness, the death toll — the ultimate price of any war — is the most difficult area in which to achieve accuracy. Canada, insulated at home from civilian bombings or military invasion, lost more than 60,000 soldiers to death and disease in the first world war, some 42, 000 in the second. A compilation of global statistics of twentieth century state violence is a sober reflection on both sacrifice and futility.

1. Russians have suffered most from war this century. Give the figure most approximating total Russian casualites from the two world wars, the purges, and the Russian Civil War.

☐ a. ten millions  ☐ b. twenty millions  ☐ c. more than fifty millions

2. Chinese have been slaughtered through invasion and internal strife. In what numbers?

☐ a. five millions    ☐ b. ten millions    ☐ c. twenty millions

3. Approximately how many died in the second world war — combatants and civilians?

4. How many people died when the Atom bomb was dropped on Hirsohima on August 6, 1945?

5. Finally, which of the following figures do you think most approximates the total number of deaths relating to conflict to this point (1987) in the twentieth-century. Include both world wars, civil wars, Asian, African, Central and South-American and Middle-eastern strife.

☐ a. 70 millions    ☐ b. 100 millions    ☐ c. more than 125 millions

# CHRISTMAS

"**C**hristmas comes but once a year," runs the old saw. This simple truth is a source of despair for most children and relief for their parents. Christmas — the day of Christ's birth — is, of course, both holy day and holiday, and is observed universally as a happy and joyous occasion. Some 105 nations throughout the world set aside December 25 as a holiday, including Canada where it is the most conspicuous and best-loved of all Canadian festivals.

The actual date of Christ's birth is unknown. Early Christians celebrated the day in secret to avoid persecution by the ancient Romans. They chose December 25, thinking it would be a safe time because it coincided roughly with the winter solstice, which had long been established as a day of celebration and formal observance by a number of pagan peoples.

The date of December 25th was formally fixed in the fourth century by the Church at Rome. The Eastern Church celebrated Christ's birth on January 6, a custom that is still followed by some Christian sects such as the Armenian church. When customs traditionally associated with Christmas are combined with church rites, and the prodigious depiction of the nativity through the ages in the visual arts, literature, drama, music, and dance, it is safe to say that Christmas is the greatest folk festival in the world. It is also without a doubt the biggest commercial holiday in the world, a trend that has been growing in this century and one which shows no sign of flagging.

A contemporary Canadian Christmas reflects the variety of Christians who form the social fabric of present-day Canada. The most commonly observed traditions and rites are those of the western church and the folk customs of France and Britain, sometimes with a modifying influence from those former British colonies to our south. However, the holiday has such power and prevalence that even non-Christians seize the occasion as a kind of all-purpose, general feast of sharing and gift-giving.

# I. NOEL

A test of bilingual understanding.  Match the French-Canadian traditions with their English counterparts.

1. messe de minuit
   ☐ a. Whence Come You, Shepherd Maiden? (hymn)

2. réveillon de Noël
   ☐ b. midnight mass

3. Père Noël
   ☐ c. The Huron Carol (hymn)

4. D'ou viens-tu, Bergère?  ☐ d. Santa Claus

5. Jésus est né
   ☐ e. follows midnight mass

## II.  OUT ON A LIMB

Find the word **XMAS** in this tree maze.  Time limit: 30 seconds.

```
                YO
               JMYU
              IPJKKA
             TJRM68UM
           TMFDSGMRTELRYL
       FHGJLKREKJTROITWEPOTJWX
      POI6PO9I54UPV9W5UJYOLI83YT
    T8I6T3598OU5BLOI8ESYTRGLIVEK4IU6
  XXXKLIJEPO9UE5HRIL8QAIWUE6OL8EBS4YE50V
U8NV9WUJ6XPY9E4SU5E5OR9VUWR7EO8US44TOE5US
POV9RYIUBSO5EIUEDPOW97UYEDPCL9NT7IUNEPON59R
IVIVJRRJ9S5UOK554UR6OY9ES5UR6POF9DU5YLYOIUEROXM
                AS
                MP
                TR
            BWKIRJMNVKRIKGK
            KRJTONJMTOHITJ5
             RUVNRMNGJTUJJ
              IIRUUEJJFKR
               RRSFDFRII
```

## III. BRITISH CHEER

1. Who was the "Lord of Misrule"?

2. Who brought the Christmas tree to England?

3. When was the first Christmas card sent?

4. On what date did the English Parliament outlaw Christmas:
☐ a. 1560      ☐ b. 1642      ☐ c. 1838

5. Why do we associate holly with Christmas?

## IV. SONGQUIZ

Identify the following Christmas carols and supply the missing lines.

1. "Hither, page, and stand by me,
   If thou know'st it, telling,
   Yonder peasant, who is he?
   Where and what his dwelling?"
   "Sire, he lives a good league hence,
   Underneath the mountain,
   Right against the forest fence,

   _____


2. 'Twas in the moon of winter time when all
   the birds had fled,
   That Mighty Gitchi Manitou sent angel choirs instead.
   Before their light the stars grew dim, and
   wand'ring hunters heard the hymn

   _____

   _____


3. Hail the heaven-born Prince of Peace!
   Hail, the Son of Righteousness!
   Light and life to all He brings,

   _____


4. Thus spake the seraph: and forthwith
   Appeared a shining throng
   Of angels praising God who thus
   Addressed their joyful ____

5. Now to the Lord sing praises,
   All you within this place,
   And with true love and brotherhood
   Each other now embrace:
   This holy tide of Christmas
   All other doth _____ .

# V. CHRISTMAS AND CANADA

1. Christmas of 1941 was a very black one for Canadians — why? What international event ocurred on that day and what was the Canadian connection?

2. Former Prime Minister Pierre Trudeau and his then wife Margaret had not one, but two sons on separate Christmas days (giving rise to much cynical, if not outright blasphemous, talk).
Can you name the boys and the years in which they were born.

3. In 1635 the man known as "the father of New France" died on Christmas day. Name him.

4. On Christmas Eve in _____, a treaty was signed in Belgium finally ending a vicious war which had been fought at least partly on Canadian territory?

5. When and where was Canada's first Christmas Tree erected?

# VI. SEASON'S GREETINGS

Match the greeting with the country of origin.

1. Glaedelig Jul    ☐ a. Spain

2. Buon Natale    ☐ b. Poland

3. Boas Festas    ☐ c. Denmark

4. Feliz Navidad    ☐ d. Finland

5. God Jul    ☐ e. France

6. Wesolych Swiat    ☐ f. Italy

7. Hauskaa Joulua    ☐ g. Norway

8. Joyeux Noel    ☐ h. Portugal and Brazil

9. Meri Kurisumasu    ☐ i. Sweden

10. Gledelig Ju    ☐ j. Japan

# VII. THE TWELVE DAYS OF CHRISTMAS

1. "On the twelfth day of Christmas, my true love gave to me". What?

2. Define Advent.

3. When and what is Epiphany?

4. Who were the Three Wise Men?

5. What gifts did they bring?

6. Why are green and red the traditional colours of Christmas?

7. When is the Feast of St. Nicholas?

8. Probably the most famous of all carols was written, composed, and performed on Christmas Eve, 1818. Name it.

9. Think of a poem, a story, a ballet, and an opera traditionally associated with Christmas.

10. *Miracle on 34th Street* is a favourite Christmas movie. Name the actor who played the Santa Claus figure.

11. The bestselling song of all time is _____, by Irving Berlin, with some 130 million records sold to date. The version sung by _____ was released in _____ and since has sold approximately _____ records.

12. What is the origin of the term boxing day?

# VIII. THE EIGHT DAYS OF HANUKKAH

Traditionally Jews do not celebrate Christmas. Instead they have a winter festival named Hanukkah which roughly coincides with the Christian feast of Christmas.

1. According to the 1981 census what proportion of the Canadian population is Jewish?

☐ a. 24.3    ☐ b. 13.6    ☐ c. 5.8    ☐ d. 1.2

2. When does the Hanukkah holiday begin?

3. Who was Judah Maccabee?

4. Why does Hanukkah last eight days?

5. What is a Hanukkah Menorah?

6. How many candles are burned during Hanukkah? Here's a hint: remember that fresh candles are used every evening.

☐ a. 9     ☐ b. 44     ☐ c. 64     ☐ d. 72

7. Which of these foods are served traditionally during Hanukkah?

☐ a. potato latkes     ☐ b. roast goose     ☐ c. sauerbraten

☐ d. fried pastries     ☐ e. gingerbread cookies     ☐ f. couscous

8. What is a dreidel?

# IX. CHRISTMAS FARE

Match the Christmas dish with the appropriate country

1. lutefisk (dried cod)     ☐ a. Sweden

2. torrone (candy)     ☐ b. Austria

3. stuffed baked carp     ☐ c. Norway

4. glogg (hot punch)     ☐ d. Mexico

5. bunuelos (pastries)     ☐ e. Italy

# X. CHRISTMAS CRACKERS

1. When and where was Canada's first Santa Claus Parade?

2. Correct the two errors in the following poem
   'Twas the day before Christmas
   When all through the house
   Not a creature was stirring
   Not even a louse.

3.  Who said:
    "I wear the chain I forged in life....I made it link by link, and yard by yard; I girded it on of my own free will, and of my own free will I wore it.

4. What peculiar incident took place in No Man's Land on Dec. 25, 1914?

5.  Unscramble the name of this Christmas Carol.  Hint:  six words are needed to "see the light".

EARMACEELHCPONUTTITIHGNDILM

# MENTAL HEALTH DAY

**S**ome holidays will never make it to the official calendar even though they occur in every season and are truly "moveable feasts." They celebrate one of the oldest human needs: a day off. Surely you recognize the scene, that morning when you roll over in bed, consider the day ahead in that airless office, ponder the interminable meeting that afternoon with that hopeless jerk from out of town, shudder at the prospect of tromping through the slush to strap-hang your way to work, and say "forget it!"

Of course the decisiveness and sheer grit exercised in making that decision is somewhat dampened by stage two: engaging in a bold-faced lie. Somebody, preferably a friend or spouse, must call work and explain that you are feeling "a bit under the weather" (a great line, but what does it mean?) or, for the more sincere, "not quite yourself — be in to-morrow." And then, truly exhausted, you tumble back into bed, deliciously contemplating the stolen joys of the day ahead.

For most of us, a little wrestle with guilt is not only inevitable, it is essential therapy. And what better place to do it than trapped in your own lodgings — after all, if you go out, somebody might spot you and inform the authorities. My advice is to snuggle down in bed with a pot of tea and a stack of well-buttered toast and read something that is good for you. Nothing fits the bill better for those of us who occupy the 49th and north than Canadiana.

So, get going, and if you find that you need a little diversion from this wholesome task, consider the following quiz. It focuses almost entirely on that wily animal CANLIT and is guaranteed to vanquish even the sharpest shards of guilt. CANLIT, which according to an uncharitable American acquaintance of mine  sounds like something used to start the barbecue, properly reflects CANSOCIETY by being bilingual and bicultural. This quiz, however, composed in darkest Toronto, explores the English side of the package only. On the other hand, solitude is spelled the same way in both languages.

# I. IN THE BEGINNING

Identify the work from which the following opening lines are taken.

1. "Northwest of Montreal, through a valley always in sight of the low mountains of the Laurentian Shield, the Ottawa River flows out of Protestant Ontario into Catholic Quebec. It comes broad and ale-colored and joins the Saint Lawrence, the two streams embrace the pan of Montreal Island, the Ottawa merges and loses itself and the mainstream moves northeastward a thousand miles to the sea."

2. "The river flowed both ways. The current moved from north to south, but the wind usually came from the south, rippling the bronze-green water in the opposite direction. This apparently impossible contradiction, made apparent and possible, still fascinated Morag, even after the years of river-watching."

3. "We slept in what had once been the gymnasium. The floor was of varnished wood, with stripes and circles painted on it, for the games that were formerly played there; the hoops for the basketball nets were still in place, though the nets were gone. A balcony ran around the room, for the spectators, and I thought I could smell, faintly like an afterimage, the pungent scent of sweat, shot through with the sweet taint of chewing gum and perfume from the watching girls, felt-skirted as I knew from pictures, later in mini-skirts, then pants, then in one earring, spiky green-streaked hair. Dances would have been held there; the music lingered, a palimpsest of unheard sound, style upon style, an undercurrent of drums, a forlorn wail, garlands made of tissue-paper flowers, cardboard devils, a revolving ball of mirrors, powdering the dancers with a snow of light."

4. "She was standing in the middle of the railroad tracks. Her head was bowed and her right front hoof was raised as if she rested. Her reins hung down to the ground and her saddle had slipped to one side. Behind her, a warehouse filled with medical supplies had just caught fire. Lying beside her there was a dog with its head between its paws and its ears erect and listening."

5. "9:05 p.m. August 9, 1972. The Coulee is so still right now that if a match were to be lit, the flame would not waver. The tall grasses stand without quivering . The tops flop this way and that. The whole dark sky is bright with stars and only the new moon moves.

We come here once every year around this time. Uncle and I. This spot is half a mile from the Barkers' farm and seven miles from the village of Granton where we finally moved in 1951.

"Nothing changes ne", I say as we walk towards the rise.

"Umi no yo," Uncle says, pointing to the grass. "It's like the sea."

# II. LITERARY OFFSPRING

Match these authors with their characters

1. Robertson Davies    ☐ a. Guido the Gimlet of Ghent

2. Stephen Leacock    ☐ b. Duddy Kravitz

3. Mordecai Richler    ☐ c. Florentine Lacasse

4. Margaret Laurence    ☐ d. Samuel Marchbanks

5. Gabrielle Roy    ☐ e. Rachel Cameron


# III. LIONS AND SHADOWS

Match the lines to the poet and the title

1.   It took the sea a thousand years,
     A thousand years to trace
     The granite features of this cliff,
     In crag and scarp and base.
     It took the sea an hour one night,
     An hour of storm to place
     The sculpture of these granite seams
     Upon a woman's face.

2.   This is the country of our defeat
     and yet
     during the plowing a man
     might stop and stand in a brown valley
     of the furrows
     and shade his eyes to watch for the same
     red patch mixed with gold
     that appears on the same
     spot in the hills
     year after year
     and grow old
     plowing and plowing a ten-acre field until
     the convolutions run parallel
     with his own brain —

3. they opn our mail petulantly
they burn down barns they cant
but they listen to our politikul
ledrs phone conversashuns what
cud b less inspiring to ovrheer

4. I said that he fell straight to the ice
where they found him.
And none but the sun and incurious
clouds have lingered
Around the marks of that day on the
ledge of the Finger,
That day, the last of my youth, on the
last of our mountains.

5. Forgot were the two shattered
porcupines
I had seen die in the bleak forest.
Pain is unreal; death, an illusion:
There is no death in all the land,
I heard my voice cry;
And brought my hand down on the butterfly
And felt the rock move beneath my hand.

☐ a. Irving Layton    ☐ b. Earle Birney    ☐ c. Al Purdy

☐ d. E.J. Pratt    ☐ e. bill bissett

☐ 1. "the wunderfulness uf the mountees, our secret police"

☐ 2. "The Country North of Belleville"

☐ 3. "Erosion"

☐ 4. "David"

☐ 5. "Butterfly on Rock"

# IV. LIT TRIV

1. James Reaney's epic trilogy *The Donellys*, comprising *Sticks and Stones*, *The St. Nicholas Hotel* and *Handcuffs*, focuses on which Ontario township?

2. Which of the following is not a Canadian publishing house?

☐ a. blewointmentpress    ☐ b. Pulp Press    ☐ c. Ragweed Press

☐ d. Tree Frog Press    ☐ e. Peter Waterhole Associates

3. Who is known as "The Cheese Poet?" To help out, here are a couple of stanzas:

> We have seen thee, queen of cheese
> Lying quietly at your ease
> Gently fanned by evening breeze,
> Thy fair form no flies dare seize . . .
>
> We'rt thou suspended from balloon,
> You'd cast a shade even at noon.
> Folks would think it was the moon
> About to fall and crush them soon.

4. Who were the 1987 winners of the Governor-General's Award for English Fiction and Poetry?

5. Before she was president of McClelland & Stewart, or the Ontario Consul in Paris, or one of the hosts of the CBC's *Fifth Estate* , Adrienne Clarkson wrote two novels. Name them.

# V. THROUGH THE PAST DARKLY

1. Who was Canada's first female novelist? As a bonus, can you give the title of her book and the year in which it was published?

2. What was John Richardson's 1832 novel *Wacousta* about?

3. Name the nineteenth-century author of ribald tales about a Yankee's smooth-talking ability to outwit Bluenosers.

4. William Kirby's most popular book was an involved melodrama focused on Intendant Bigot's New France. What was the name of the novel and, as a bonus, in what year was it published?

5. Sara Jeanette Duncan wrote of the cultural distinctions among Britons, Canadians and Americans. What 1904 novel, set in a southern Ontario town, best expresses her pre-occupation with the then significant question of Imperial unity? For an extra point, what were the fictional and real names of the town she was writing about?

# VI. (MOSTLY) LITERARY KNIGHTS

1. Name the bestselling Canadian historical novelist who was also a British MP, a Knight Baronet, married to a New York heiress, and during the first world war, in charge of the British Propaganda campaign to get America into the war.

2. Identify the New Brunswick-born poet and novelist with more than 50 volumes to his credit, who lived and wrote in New York and Britain before settling in Toronto in 1925.

3. A literary and social critic, he was also Professor of the History of Medicine at McGill University, a physican, official historian of the Canadian Medical Services in the first world war and Editor of the *University Magazine*, from 1907 to 1920. Who was he?

4. Name the bilingual Quebec lawyer and civil servant who was the author of the popular set of six miscellanies entitled *Maple Leaves* (1863-1906)

5. Best-known as an archeologist and early anthropologist and President of the University of Toronto, he also taught English Literature and ran *The Canadian Journal* where he is said to have "established academic literary criticism in the Canadas."

# VII. SECOND DEBUT

Although there are many examples such as Hugh MacLennan's *Two Solitudes* or Leonard Cohen's *Beautiful Losers* where a second novel is widely applauded, it is usually first novels which grab all the attention. Match the writer with the title of his or her second novel (the first is in parentheses).

1. Earle Birney (*Turvey*)
2. Morley Callaghan (*Strange Fugitive*)
3. Sinclair Ross (*As for Me and My House*)
4. Ernest Buckler (*The Mountain and the Valley*)
5. Brian Moore (*The Lonely Passion of Judith Hearne*)

☐ a. *It's Never Over*       ☐ b. *The Well*

☐ c. *The Cruelest Month*    ☐ d. *Down the Long Table*

☐ e. *The Feast of Lupercal*

# VIII. SCRAMBLE

Unscramble the following to discover a book title. For an extra point, name the author. Here's a scrambled clue: A aesft fo npteseh

CARDIAAN HTIW RIHC EILD EHT NEDASERUTV

# IX. POOR AND WELL-KNOWN

Match these authors with their other careers.

1. Raymond Souster     ☐ a. Clergyman

2. Duncan Campbell Scott     ☐ b. Bank Clerk

3. Robert Service     ☐ c. Bank Clerk

4. Ralph Connor     ☐ d. Actor

5. Gordon Pinsent     ☐ e. Civil Servant

# X. WHO AM I?

Identify the speakers.

1. "I am not a great poet and I never was. Greatness in poetry must proceed from greatness of character, from force, fearlessness, brightness, I have none of these qualities. I am, if anything, the very opposite. I am weak; I am a coward. I am a hypochondriac. I am a minor poet of a superior order and that is all." (1895)

2. "Under the avalanche of manuscripts the sorrowful conviction was forced upon me, that in my youthful innocence — I was not yet sixty — I had been mistaken all the while: the chief industry of Canada was not agriculture; it was writing; six out of its eight million English-speaking citizens dreamed of literary fame." (1938)

3. "To be a Jew and a Canadian is to emerge from the ghetto twice, for self-conscious Canadians, like some touchy Jews, tend to contemplate the world through a wrong-ended telescope, as witness what is still my most cherished Canadian newspaper headline: 1960 WAS A GOOD YEAR FOR PLAYWRIGHTS FROM OUTSIDE CANADA." (1968)

4. "I myself talk Ontario English: I don't admire it, but it's all I can do; anything is better than affectation." (1938)

5. "I write poems like spiders spin webs, and perhaps for much the same reason: to support my existence." (1972)

Choose from: E.J. Pratt, Al Purdy, Archibald Lampman, Stephen Leacock, Frederick Philip Grove, E. Pauline Johnson, Emily Carr , Mordecai Richler, and Norman Levine.

# XI. SCRAMBLE (II)

Arrange the letters in the following anagrams so that they spell the last names of five well-known Canadian novelists. Then take the third letter of each unscrambled name to form the name of a sixth novelist.

ENRRAG

SADIEV

GNEEL

EEIBW

OERMO

# XII. NAMING NUMBERS AND NUMBERING NAMES

Count the letters in the first and last name of the "Confederation Poet" who, in 1927, edited the first Oxford Book of AmericanVerse. Add the number of letters in the title of the most famous Canadian poem of the first world war. Divide by the number of letters in the first and last names of the author of Anatomy of Criticism. Subtract one from the remainder. How many solitudes do you have left?

# New Year's Day Answers

## I. FIRST THINGS LAST

1. Janus was guardian of the gates and doorways including the portal opening the new year. He was double-faced, it was thought, because the gate opened both ways and he looked back into the past and ahead to the future.
2. January 13, by the Gregorian calendar.
3. 1. Cameroon; 2. Haiti; 3. Sudan
4. b. William the Conqueror tried to initiate the practice, but England soon slipped back into celebrating what was the traditional European date of March 25 — which lasted largely until the adoption of the Gregorian Calendar in 1582 by Roman Catholic countries. Scotland adopted the January 1 date shortly thereafter, but England did not do so officially until 1752 during the reign of George II.
5. The new year began with the heliacal rising of Sirius, which itself coincided with the beginning of the flood of the Nile River.
6. Vietnam. The day, as in China, falls on the Lunar new year and is thus moveable.
7. d. Big Ben boomed on 31 December, 1923 — on New Year's eve.
8. Samuel Pepys.
9. a. 1959; b. Fidel Castro; c. Fulgencio Batista; d. Cuba.
10. 1. c ; 2. e; 3. a; 4. b; 5. d.

## II. NEW YEAR'S DAY IN THE TRUE NORTH

1. Quebec City; 2. Rocky Mountains; 3. 1947; 4. Ottawa; 5. 1922

## III. CANADIAN FIRSTS

1. b. 1871, pop. 3,635,024
2. b. The Champlain and Saint Lawrence Railway ran from Laprairie on the St. Lawrence to St. Johns on the Richelieu River and opened as a portage route on July 21, 1836.
3. b. In 1734 a special messenger was appointed to carry official despatches between Montreal and Quebec. For an additional fee he would carry personal messages. The first official post office in Canada was established by Benjamin Leigh in Halifax in 1754. Benjamin Franklin, then a loyal subject of King George, established the Post Office at Quebec in 1763.
4. c. The Threepenny Beaver, designed by Sandford Fleming, was issued on April 23, 1851. It was the world's first pictorial stamp.
5. b. *The Halifax Gazette*, first issued on March 23, 1752, by John Bushnell.
6. b. J.A.D. McCurdy flew the Silver Dart on February 23, 1909. He was an associate of Alexander Graham Bell, inventor of the telephone, who had backed the planning and execution of the flight.
7. c. In 1935, at least in part because of difficulties brought about controlling the depression.

**8.** a. It first was introduced into the Province of Canada (now Ontario and Quebec) in 1858 and was based on a dollar equal in value to the American one.

**9.** c. George ORTON (1873-1958) in 1900. Canada did not have an official team so he entered with the U. S. team to win the 400 metre hurdles.

**10.** c. The games were first held in Canada, in Hamilton, Ontario in August, 1930. 400 competitors attended from 11 countries.

## IV. WOMEN FIRST AND FOREMOST

1, D, vi; 2, A, x; 3, B, iii; 4, C, ix; 5, E, vii; 6, F, i or iv; 7, G, v; 8, J, i or iv; 9, I, viii; 10, H, ii

## V. BEGINNING WITH A BANG

Frederick **Banting**, picture C, won the prize for medicine, together with J.J.R. Macleod (Scottish) for their discovery of insulin in 1923.

Lester **Pearson**, picture D, won for peace in 1957, because of his work temporizing the Suez Crisis in 1956.

Gerhard **Herzberg**, picture B , won the chemistry prize for his work on molecular spectroscopy in 1971.

John **Polanyi**, picture. A, together with Dudley Herschback and Yuan Tseh Lee (both of the United States), won the prize in Chemistry for their work on crossed molecular beams (which helps explain how chemical reactions take place).

## VI. BEGINNING WITH A BANG (PART II)

Jamaican-born Canadian sprinter Ben Johnson, on August 30, 1987, in a meet in Rome, Italy, set the world 100-metre track record at 9.83 seconds.

# ALL SAINTS DAZE ANSWERS

## I. SAINTS BE PRAISED

1. d, iii; 2. b, i; 3. a, iv; 4. e, v; 5. c, ii

## II. OTHER WAYS, OTHER DAYS I

1.c; 2.a; 3.b; 4.e; 5.d

## III. WHO AM I?

1. St. David patron saint of Wales
2. St. Patrick, patron saint of Ireland
3. St. George, patron saint of England
4. St. Andrew, patron saint of Scotland.

# IV. OTHER WAYS, OTHER DAYS II

**1.** f, ix; **2.** j, iii; **3.** h, vii or viii; **4.** a, vii or viii; **5.** b, x; **6.** c, i; **7.** d, vi; **8.** e, ii; **9.** i, iv; **10.** g, v

# V. ALL SAINTS MAZE

**a.** St. George; **b.** St. Patrick, **c.** St. Andrew, **d.** St. David

# VI. DAILY DIVERSITY

**1.** b and d.
**2.** Legend says that when she was put on a spiked wheel to break her faith, the wheel itself broke and she was unhurt while some spectators were killed by flying splinters. She was eventually beheaded and from her severed veins milk flowed rather than blood.
**3.** It is celebrated on February 6 in New Zealand to commemorate the signing of a peace treaty in 1840 between Britain and the Maori chiefs.
**4.** Leap year occurs once every four years when February has an extra day.
**5.** none of them — April Fool.

# VII. VEDDY ENGLISH

**1.** William Shakespeare
**2.** Rupert Brooke
**3.** J.M.W. Turner
**4.** William Wordsworth

# VIII. HIGH AND HOLY DAYS I

**1.** The cross represents the crucifixion of Jesus Christ and his victory over death.
**2.** Lamb is a traditional Easter food and often cookies and cakes shaped like lambs decorate Easter tables. The symbol of the lamb comes from the Jewish festival of Passover when a lamb was sacrificed during a Passover ceremony in the Temple in Jerusalem. The Christians interpreted the sacrifice as a harbinger of Christ's crucifixion — "Jesus is the lamb of God who taketh away the sins of the world."
**3.** In some countries Roman Catholics put out all the lights in their churches on Good Friday. On Easter Saturday they make a new fire to light the paschal or Easter candle, which is then used to light all the candles in the church.
**4.** The new life that returns to nature about Eastertime. Although the Egyptians and Perisans often dyed eggs in spring colours and gave them to friends as gifts, the early Christians of Mesopotamia were the first to use coloured eggs for Easter.
**5.** The childhood belief that an Easter bunny brings Easter eggs probably comes from a German legend in which a poor woman dyed eggs during a famine and hid them in a nest as an Easter gift for her children. Just as the children discovered the nest, a big rabbit hopped away thus giving rise to the legend that it was the rabbit who brought the eggs.

## IX. HIGH AND HOLY DAYS II

1. It begins in March or April on the 15th day of the Hebrew month of Nisan and lasts eight days, although Israelis and Reform Jews celebrate for seven.
2. The word Passover comes from the Biblical story of the tenth plague which God brought on Egypt for keeping the Israelites in bondage. God killed the first born child in every Egyptian home, but passed over the homes of the Israelites.
3. A ceremonial feast to celebrate Passover.
4. Unleavened bread. According to the Bible when the Israelites fled, they did not have time to let their bread rise and so they made flat unleavened bread called matzohs instead.

## X. TRICK OR TREAT

1. d; 2. e; 3. b; 4. c; 5. a.

# Victoria Day Answers

## I. CROWNED HEADS

1. 1819
2. April 21, 1926
3. 1.c; 2.b; 3.a; 4.d; 5.e.
4. c. Since 1960 the family name has offically been Mountbatten-Windsor.
5. c. Meredith. Debrett's Peerage explains that Henry VII took the name Tudor from his grandfather Owen Tudor who was also known as Owen Meredith. They go on to suggest had he taken the other name Britain would now be dotted with "Ye Olde Meredith Tea Rooms."
6. George V. The German name was dropped in 1917 and replaced with the very British Windsor. The Kaiser is reported to have said that thereafter, in the German Empire, all performances of "The Merry Wives of Windsor" were to be called "The Merry Wives of Saxe-Cobourg and Gotha."
7. Technically, the Heir Apparent is the "heir male of the body of the reigning sovereign." A female could only be Heir Apparent if a male Heir Apparent were to die within the lifetime of the sovereign bearing only female children. She would be known as Heiress Apparent. The Heir Presumptive is the next person in line to a sovereign who has no male heir. The present queen was Heiress Presumptive; the Heir Apparent to the throne at present is, of course, Prince Charles.
8. They are already in the right order. The appropriate dates are:

1. William I    1027?-1087
2. Richard I    1157-1199
3. Edward I    1239-1272
4. James I    1566-1625
5. Charles I    1600-1649
6. George I    1660-1727

**9.** e. Clarence House is the London residence of the Queen Mother.
**10.** In 1939, when George VI and his wife Elizabeth, the present Queen Mother, visited the country.

## II. FLAGS AND SYMBOLS

**1. A.** Ont; **B.** N.S.; **C.** N. B.; **D.** B.C.; **E.** Quebec; **F.** Nfld.; **G.** P.E. I.; **H.** Alberta
**2.**
I,      F, 5
II,     C, 6
III,    H, 1
IV,     E, 7
V,      B, 2
VI,     A, 4
VII,    G, 8
VIII,   D, 3
**3.** The Arms of Canada.
**4.** The verbal description in heraldic language is called a blazon. The pictorial depiction is known as the emblazonment.
**5.** c. the beaver, symbol of Canada
**6.** It was proclaimed by Parliament on 15 February, 1965.
**7.** d. all of the above
**8.** c .thirty-seven
**9.** c. 210
**10.** It comes from the Bible. Psalms 72:8 reads "He shall have dominion also from sea to sea, and from the river unto the ends of the earth."

## III. VICE-REGAL CANADA

**1.** 1, A, f; **2**, H, b; **3**, G, c; **4**, J, d; **5**, C, j; **6**, B, g; **7**, I, i; **8**, F, h; **9**, E, e; **10**, D, a
**2.** Governor-General Earl Grey donated the Grey Cup for excellence in football in 1909.
**3.** Georges Vanier
**4.** a. The Marquess of Lorne (1844-1914), Governor-General from 1878-1883, married Queen Victoria's fourth daughter, Princess Louise, in 1871. He also founded the Royal Society of Canada.
**5.** The Duke of Connaught (1850-1942), was the third (and, incidentally, the favourite) son of Queen Victoria.
**6.** John Buchan, Lord Tweedsmuir. His best-known work is probably *The Thirty-Nine Steps* (1915).
**7.** a. Vincent Massey
**8.** c. Pauline McGibbon of Ontario was the first to read the Speech from the Throne — in 1974.
**9.** Ralph G. Steinhauer, farmer and Indian leader, became Lieutenant-Governor of Alberta in 1974 and served for five years.
**10.** G.F.G. Stanley was the person who provided the basic design for the Maple Leaf Flag.

## IV. THE ROYAL US AND THEM

1.  Elizabeth I. "I will make you shorter by a head." [Ref. Chamberlin, *Sayings of Queen Elizabeth*].
2.  Charles II. "Let not poor Nelly starve." [said of the actress Nell Gwynne, evidently on his deathbed].
3.  Edward VIII. "I have found it impossible . . . to discharge my duties as king . . . without the help and support of the woman I love." [from his Abdication broadcast, 11 December, 1936].
4.  Victoria. "We are not amused." [Ref. *Notebooks of a Spinster Lady*, 2 Jan., 1900].
5.  Henry II. "Who will free me from this turbulent priest?"
[attributed to Henry II in reference to Thomas à Becket, Archbishop of Canterbury].


# Canada Day Answers

## I. 1860s

1.  In 1861 two Confederate agents were removed from the British mail packet *Trent* by the captain of the American USS *San Jacinto*. A war scare resulted and 15,000 British troops were sent to Canada. The United States eventually released the southerners and the crisis passed.
2.  g. Cartieria
3.  The Fenians were a group of Irish-Americans organized in the 1850s to help secure Irish independence from Britain. One faction tried to foment an uprising in Ireland, while another, led by William Roberts, carried out several raids into the British colonies that have since become Canada.
4.  Riel had trained for the priesthood, served as a law clerk in Montreal, and held various odd jobs.
5.  *Das Kapital* by Karl Marx.

## II. 1870s

1.  1873
2.  The full title of *Erewhon* (actually an anagram rather than a backward spelling) is *Erewhon or Over the Range*.
3.  Stonemason.
4.  b. 3.5 million
5.  Alexander Graham Bell. The significance, in his own words, was that the event marked "the first transmission of speech to a distance."

## III 1880s

1.  The Royal Society of Canada, the senior national organization of distinquished Canadian scholars.
2.  Charles "Chinese" Gordon, trapped at Khartoum.
3.  Honoré Mercier.
4.  James A. Garfield succeeded by Chester Arthur.
5.  *The Gondoliers*

## IV 1890s

1.  Sir John Abbott who took office in 1891.
2.  The Victorian Order of Nurses.
3.  b. Abbott, 1891-2; c. Thompson, 1892-4; d. Bowell, 1894-6; a. Tupper, April to July, 1896.
4.  These three gentlemen struck gold at Rabbit (later, appropriately Bonanza) Creek, a tributary of the Klondike River, in the Yukon in August, 1896. It was the beginning of the Klondike Gold Rush.
5.  Lester B. Pearson.

## V 1900s

1.  Frank.
2.  Five-pin bowling.
3.  William Lyon Mackenzie King.
4.  1903.
5.  Louis Blériot.

## VI 1910s

1.  1915 in *Punch*.
2.  c. 72
3.  The sinking of *The Empress of Ireland* after a collision with the Norwegian collier *Storstad* with a death toll of 1,024.
4.  *Mont Blanc*.
5.  The official opening of the Panama Canal.

## VII 1920s

1.  Benares, an 1837 house in Clarkson, Ontario, now under the jurisdiction of the Ontario Heritage Foundation.
2.  In 1923 during the first play-by-play broadcast of a hockey game between the Kitchener Seniors and Parkdale Canoe Club at the Mutual Street Arena in Toronto. Hewitt made his broadcast from the penalty box.

**3.** The Chanak incident in 1922 when Canada did not automatically rush to Britain's aid against Turkish insurgents, and the signing of the Halibut Treaty of 1923 when for the first time Canadians signed a foreign treaty without the representation of the mother country.

**4.** 1926.

**5.** Babe Ruth.

## VIII 1930s

**1.** Dr. Alan Roy Dafoe. The quints were Annette, Emilie, Yvonne, Cécile, and Marie.

**2.** Department store owner John David Eaton.

**3.** "King or Chaos".

**4.** 1.c; 2.b; 3.d; 4.e; 5.a.

**5.** Essentially it was the initial platform of the Co-operative Commonwealth Federation as revised at the Regina Conference of the party in August, 1933. Central was the phrase "The principle regulating production, distribution and exchange will be the supplying of human needs and not the making of profits...." Clarence Peterson, the father of the present premier of Ontario, David Peterson, was one of the signatories.

## IX 1940s

**1.** The Unemployment Insurance Act came into force.

**2.** Hong Kong.

**3.** 1948.

**4.** Charlotte Whitton in *Saturday Night* Jan. 26, 1946.

**5.** Fewer than 5,000.

## X 1950s

**1.** Cavazzi.

**2.** Alec Guinness as Richard III. Amelia Hall, playing Queen Anne, was the first Canadian and also the first woman.

**3.** 1. **d** or e; 2. **c**; 3. d or e; 4. b; 5. a.

**4.** *Front Page Challenge* which started in 1957.

**5.** 1956.

## XI 1960s

**1.** John Diefenbaker in Winnipeg, March 4, 1963.

**2.** Saskatchewan.

**3.** b. a furry Arctic owl doll

**4.** downhill slalom.

**5.** a. Unilateral Declaration of Independence (Rhodesia's break from the United Kingdom, 1965); b. Five Basic Exercises for Me (a popular exercise book published by the RCAF, 1960); c. Rassemblement pour l'Independance Nationale (the first separatist party of this generation in Quebec, 1960); **d**. Company of Young Canadians (Canada's domestic peace corps, 1966); **e**. *That Was The Week That Was* (or commonly *TW3*, a British satirical TV program).

## XII 1970s

1. The 1976 battle over the right to communicate in French on aircraft operating through Quebec airfields. In retrospect it is thought that the divisions over this issue contributed to the victory of the Parti Québécois in Quebec in 1976.
2. Jérôme Choquette.
3. 1.e,1970; 2.d,1971; 3.c,1972; 4.b,1973; 5.a,1974.
4. c. Things first got together in the 1960s.
5. d. $800 million. The roof was a bargain at $117 million.

## XIII 1980s

1. Saturday, June 11, 1983 when Joe Clark lost the Tory leadership to Brian Mulroney.
2. Pierre Elliott Trudeau in January, 1980 during the election campaign of that year.
3. Approximately $24 million.
4. c. The Progressive Conservatives won 211 seats of a possible 282.
5. William Davis of Ontario, René Lévèsque of Quebec, and Peter Lougheed of Alberta.

# Civic Holiday Answers

## I.    DEFINITIONS

1. a. a variety of salmon found in northern waters.
2. b. a Quebec conservative
3. c. the high tide that enters the Bay of Fundy
4. c. a fermented bread dough used in rough baking
5. b. a West Coast Indian celebration
6. b. an edible fern
7. c. a dark, rough Newfoundland rum
8. c. a warm wind in Western Canada
9. b. sections of land set aside for the support and maintenance of the Protestant Clergy
10. c. a derisive nickname for the old narrow-gauge Newfoundland train

## II.    NAME THAT PLACE

1.d; 2.f; 3.g; 4.a; 5.j; 6.h; 7.i; 8.e; 9.b; 10.c.

## III.   SCRAMBLE

1.   Thompson
2.   Diefenbaker
3.   Bennett
4.   Borden
5.   St. Laurent

o e n r L = Marquess of Lorne, Governor General 1878~1883

## IV.   THE PEOPLES' PALACES

A. B.C;  B. P.E.I.;  C. Ontario;  D. Newfoundland;  E. Saskatchewan;  F. Alberta;  G. N. B.;  H. Nova Scotia;  I. Quebec;  J. Manitoba

## V.   PROVINCIAL RIGHTS

1.   c.Sir Charles Tupper (1864)
2.   c.Alexander Mackenzie (1874)
3.   a.Goldwin Smith (1878)

## VI.   CIVIC MONUMENTS

1.   Montreal (Mark Twain)
2.   Ottawa (Sir Charles G. D. Roberts)
3.   Halifax (Rudyard Kipling)
4.   Toronto (Anna Jameson)
5.   Quebec City (Rupert Brooke)

## VII.   STREETSMARTS

1.   Toronto
2.   Montreal
3.   Quebec City
4.   Vancouver
5.   Winnipeg
6.   Ottawa
7.   Halifax
8.   Regina
9.   Edmonton
10.  Victoria

## VIII.  THE MOSTEST

1.   A trick question. By area, Timmins, Ontario is largest at 3,004.39 sq. km.
2.   Mount Logan in the Yukon at 5,951 metres.
3.   westernmost

4. Baffin Island at 507,451 square km.
5. The Mackenzie with a length of 4,241 km.

## IX. GOING TO EXTREMES

1. On February 3, 1947 the temperature at Snag, Yukon dropped to -63 degrees centigrade.
2. On July 5, 1937 a reading of 45 degrees centigrade was made at Midale, Saskatchewan.
3. Victoria, B. C. with a mean annual temperature of 10.4 degrees centigrade.
4. The aptly-named Ocean Falls, B. C. where 438.68 cm. drop every year.
5. Argentia, Newfoundland, has fog 56% of the time — 206 days a year on average.

## X. POP CULTURE

1. Prince Edward Island has a population per square kilometre of 22.6 persons. The national figure is 2.8.
2. Italian at 2.2 % of the population (527,000).
3. According to the 1981 census c. 491, 460.
4. 60 years for males and 62.1 years for females.
5. Almost totlally reversed. According to the 1981 census 75.7% of the Canadian population is urban and 24.3 % is rural.

## XI. SIGHTSEEING

1. west coast of Newfoundland
2. Prince Edward Island
3. Cape Breton Island, Nova Scotia
4. New Brunswick
5. Montreal, Quebec
6. Ontario
7. Kingston, Ontario
8. near Sault Ste. Marie, Ontario
9. Winnipeg, Manitoba
10. near Prince Albert, Saskatchewan
11. along the Red deer River in southeast Alberta
12. Edmonton, Alberta
13. Vancouver Island, B.C.
14. Dawson City, Yukon
15. Moncton, New Brunswick

## XII. ONE GAME AT A TIME

1. Saddledome
2. Canadian football
3. The running of The Queen's Plate horse race in Toronto.
4. You would have been the most "sportsmanlike" hockey player in the National Hockey League.
5. Skateboarding.

# Labour Day Answers

## I. WORKING LANGUAGE

1.b; 2.e; 3.d; 4.c; 5.a

## II. UNION LABELS

**a.** a worker, who refuses to join a union or to go on strike, especially a worker who crosses a picket line to take the place of a striker.
**b.** a person acting or employed as a thug(either by management or Labour) to commit acts of violence or intimidation.
**c.** a British version of a scab.
**d.** a shirker or loafer, particularly one who makes excuses to avoid work .
**e.** one who does menial work or, more commonly now, an assistant or apprentice.

## III. STRIKES

1.j; 2.b; 3.i; 4.g; 5.c; 6.h; 7.a; 8.e; 9.f; 10.d.

## IV.SHORTCUTS

1.Confederation Générale du Travail. French, founded 1895, approximately 2.5 million members.
2.American Federation of Labor-Congress of Industrial Organizations, founded 1955, 14,066,000 members.
3.Trades Union Congress. British, founded 1868, 11,515,920 members.
4.Canadian Labour Congress, Canadian, founded 1956, 2,043,484 members.
5.International Confederation of Free Trade Unions, founded 1949, 53,022,329 members.
6.World Confederation of Labour, founded 1920, 14,543,820 members.
7.World Federation of Trade Unions, founded 1945, 160,000,000 members.
8.All Union Central Council of Trade Unions, Soviet, founded 1918, 107,000,000 members.
9.International Labour Organization. Founded 1919.
10. Possibly the world's largest union—at least in terms of its name: The International Association of Marble, Slate and Stone Polishers, Rubbers and Sawyers, Tile and Marble Setters' Helpers and Marble, Mosaic, and Terrazzo Workers' Helpers.

## V. LEADING ROLES

1.i; 2.c; 3.j; 4.d; 5.e; 6.b; 7.h; 8.a; 9.g; 10.f.

## VI. DEFINITIONS

1.    b.  Cost of Living Adjustment

2. c. Practice of limiting wage increases to select personnel
3. c. Working at another job in addition to regular work
4. c. Work efficiency analysis
5. b. a part-time or temporary worker
6. b. Unofficial strikes
7. c. Payment awarded according to amount of work done
8. b. Qualified artisan who works for another
9. c. Factory employing unskilled labour at low, low pay
10. c. The creation of unnecessary work to earn more money

## VII. BEAVER TALES (I)

1.b; 2.a; 3.e; 4.c; 5.d

## VIII. BEAVER TALES (II)

1. George Brown, editor of The *Globe*.
2. 19%; in 1933.
3. 1940.
4. influential Communist leader in the "On to Ottawa" trek of 1935.
5. William Lyon Mackenzie.
6. William Lyon Mackenzie King and Pierre Elliott Trudeau.
7. The OBU or One Big Union was a movement founded in Calgary in 1919 whose aims were to unite workers in one large trade union to replace the old craft unions.
8. 1. CUPE, 304, 269 members; 2. NUPGE, 254,278 members; 3, CAW, 140,000 members.
9. A matter of some debate, but the first recognizably modern unions were probably formed in Toronto in the 1860s and 1870s. The Toronto Trades Assembly was established in 1871.
10. "Seventy-five cents a day and all the beer they want to drink."

## IX.BEAVER TALES (III)

1.e; 2.d; 3.b; 4.a; 5.c.

## X. POTPOURRI

1. According to the *Guinness Book of World Records* , the longest recorded strike was among barbers' assistants in Copenhagen. It ended Jan. 4, 1961 after 33 years.
2. Switzerland, not surprisingly. In December, 1973 the total unemployed population (in a country of 6.6 million) was reported at 81.
3. *Norma Rae*
4. The Wobblies was a popular name given to the IWW, the Industrial Workers of the World, a revolutionary union organized in Chicago in 1905. Its aim was to unite in a single body all workers to overthrow capitalism and rebuild on a socialist basis.
5. Robert White

# Thanksgiving Answers

1. e and f. Neither baron of beef nor plum pudding would likely have been eaten by the early Puritans at a Thanksgiving meal. Celebrating Christmas was considered a Catholic affectation and so such "superstitious meats" as baron of beef, boar's head, plum-pudding and mince pie, associated with Christ's Mass, were discarded in favour of indigenous foods such as turkey, other wild game, and pumpkins.

2. American Thanksgiving is always the fourth Thursday of November.

3. If so, only accidentally. The general explanation for the earlier Canadian date is the earlier Canadian harvest.

4. 1.b; 2.e; 3.a; 4.c; 5.d.

5. The last sheaf of the harvest grain, dressed up to appear as a woman — usually in a dress and with ribbons.

6. Armistice (later Remembrance) Day, from 1921 to 1931, was celebrated on the same date as Thanksgiving.

7. Governor William Bradford of Plymouth Colony in New England presided over an event that lasted three days.

8. During the American Civil War, in 1863. Credit is usually given to Sarah J. Hale, a Boston editor, who bombarded successive administrations with her view that a national day of thanksgiving would have religious qualities and also unify the country. Abraham Lincoln responded to her entreaties. Thanksgiving is the oldest national holiday celebrated in the United States.

9. The event marked the end of Britain's war with Napoleon's France.

10. Some scholars suggest that at their first thanksgiving in 1621, the American Pilgrim Fathers were consciously imitating Sukkoth, the nine-day Jewish harvest festival. It is customary at this time for families to hold meals in a sukkah or small hut decorated with flowers, fruit and branches. In contemporary society, family sukkahs frequently have been replaced by one large symbolic sukkah to be used by an entire congregation.

# Remembrance Day Answers

## I. CANADA AT WAR

1. d. King Philip was a sachem of the Wampanoag Indians in New England who led a series of attacks against English settlements in the late seventeenth century. He was killed in August of 1676 by another Indian in the service of the colonists.

2. 1. d; 2. a; 3. b; 4. c; 5. e.

3. 1. c; 2. b; 3. b; 4. c; 5. c.

4. The St. Alban's Raid of October 19, 1864 saw a group of Confederates raid St. Alban's, Vermont, from their safe base across the Canadian border. The town was shot up, three banks robbed, and one man killed. Americans were highly indignant (and rightly so) and the event spurred the delegates at Quebec, then considering a possible Canadian Confederation, to get on with their job.

**5.** The Battle of Chrysler's Farm occurred on November 11, 1813. 4000 American troops were defeated by a force of about 800 British regulars, Canadian militia and loyal Indians. The site is near Morrisburg, Ontario, on the St. Lawrence.

## II. OTHER TIMES AND PLACES

**d.** The *Tirpitz* was sunk on November 12, 1944.

## III. OTHER TIMES AND PLACES II

1. St. Martin is the Patron Saint of reformed drunkards.
2. Nat Turner
3. Jamaica
4. Typhoid Mary was a carrier of the dreaded disease who frequently acted as a cook in restaurants and institutions. It is thought more than fifty people died as a result of coming into contact with her.
5. The Italians at Taranto.

## IV. BELLIGERENT WORDS

1. b. Laurier was speaking in the House of Commons in Ottawa on August 19, 1914 at the beginning of the first world war.
2. Pierre Trudeau regarding the FLQ crisis in the autumn of 1970.
3. Joseph Goebbels, the Nazi propaganda chief, in his diary in the spring of 1943.
4. b. The Prime Minister was speaking about the highly-charged topic in the House of Commons on June 10, 1942.
5. b. Captain Arthur Roy Brown in a letter to his father written April 27, 1918, six days after his exploit.

## V. MORE BELLIGERENT WORDS

1. e; 2. a; 3. c; 4. d; 5. b.

## VI. WORDS AT WAR

1. b; 2. c; 3. e; 4. d; 5. a.

## VII. PACTS

1. d. Germany, Austria-Hungary and Russia
2. b.
3. c. Germany, Austria-Hungary and Italy
4. e. Bavaria, Wurtemberg, Hesse-Darmstadt, Baden and twelve other German territories united under the protection of Napoleon.
5. a. Britain and France

## VIII. PAX

1. Appomatox; 2. Versailles; 3. Maginot; 4. Vereeniging; 5. war-war.

## IX.WAR POETRY

1. Rupert Brooke in "The Soldier"
2. Siegfried Sassoon's Armistice peom, "Everyone Sang"
3. Wilfred Owen in "Dulce et Decorum Est"
4. Robert Graves in "Recalling War"
5. Edmund Blunden in "Report on Experience"

## X. CANADA AT WAR II

1. The sculptor was Walter S. Allward of Toronto. His design was one of 160 submitted. The work began in 1925 and was completed 11 years later. The monument was dedicated by King Edward VIII on July 26, 1936.
2. The heavily-fortified ridge was captured by the Canadian Corps — 100,000 strong — on Easter Monday (April 9, 1917). 150 guns and mortars were taken, the front-line moved three miles, and 4,000 Germans made prisoner. The cost: 3598 Canadian lives.
3. 11, 285 names of Canadian soldiers who died in France, but who have no known graves are carved on the base.
4. Lord Beaverbrook
5. "In Flander's Fields" by Lieutenant Colonel John McCrae.

## XI.THE PRICE OF WAR

1. c. More than fifty millions
2. c. Twenty millions
3. More than fifty millions has been estimated.
4. At least 80,000 dead instantly. Estimates suggest the final death toll from after-effects amounted to well over 90,000.
5. c. More than 125 millions

# Christmas Answers

## I. NOEL

1.b; 2.e; 3.d; 4.a; 5.c.

## II. OUT ON A LIMB

The first two letters XM on the far right of the bottom branch are followed by AS on the first part of the visible trunk.

## III. BRITISH CHEER

1. In the late middle ages, a peasant or servant would be chosen to be the ruler of the Christmas season. Almost always this "rule" got out of hand, and much frivolity and laughter resulted. Some think the custom originated in the Roman Saturnalia when slaves were given equal status to their masters.
2. Although some trace the tree to Druidic days, credit for our contemporary use is usuallly given to Albert, the Prince Consort, (Queen Victoria's husband) who introduced a number of German Christmas conventions to Britain.
3. "Sent" is the operative word. The practice came into effect after the introduction of the penny post in Britain in 1840. J. C. Horsley of the Royal Academy made the first card of which some 1000 copies were sold. By the 1860s the custom had become widespread.
4. b. Christmas was outlawed at the height of puritan influence in 1642, when it was decreed by parliament that "no observance shall be had, nor any solemnity used or excercised in Churches . . . " Christmas (happily) was itself restored with "the Restoration" in 1660.
5. The bringing of holly into the house was an ancient Druid custom relating to the solstice. Holly has its origins, not surprisingly, in Holy; the Druid practice was to bring sprigs of it inside as a warm winter refuge for woodland spirits

## IV. SONGQUIZ

1. Good King Wenceslas
   By Saint Agnes' Fountain
2. The Huron Christmas Carol (by Jean de Brébeuf)
   Jesus, your King is born./ Jesus is born: in excelsis gloria.
3. Hark! The Herald Angels Sing
   Risen with healing in His wings.
4. While Shepherds Watched
   song
5. God Rest You Merry, Gentlemen
   efface.

## V. CHRISTMAS AND CANADA

1. a. The Hong Kong garrison surrendered to the Japanese that day after bitter fighting. 2,000 Canadian troops had been sent to reinforce the British forces there; more than a quarter of them died either in the fighting or later in prison camps.
2. Justin was born Christmas Day, 1971; Sacha was born two years later on the same day in 1973.
3. Samuel de Champlain.
4. 1814. The War of 1812 fought between Britain and the United States was concluded by the Treaty of Ghent. Interestingly, the Battle of New Orleans was fought after the peace had been signed.

**5.** It is thought that Baron von Riedesel (1738-1800) erected the first Canadian Christmas tree at Sorel, on the St. Lawrence between Montreal and Quebec on December 24, 1781.

## VI. SEASON'S GREETINGS

1.c; 2.f; 3.h; 4.a; 5.i; 6.b; 7.d; 8.e; 9.j; 10.g.

## VII. THE TWELVE DAYS OF CHRISTMAS

**1.** During the twelve days of Christmas the true love sent:
Twelve lords a-leaping, eleven ladies dancing,
Ten pipers piping, nine drummers drumming,
Eight maids a-milking, seven swans a-swimming,
Six geese a-laying, five gold rings,
Four calling birds, three French hens,
Two turtle doves, and
A partridge in a pear tree.

**2.** Advent is the Sunday closest to November 30th, the Feast of St. Andrew. It marks the beginning of the four week period preceding Christmas. Many people observe Advent by making a wreath of holly or evergreen. To mark each Sunday of Advent a dark purple candle is added to the wreath. On the third Sunday, custom dictates that a pink candle be added to mark the beginning of the second half of Advent. On Christmas Day a large red candle is added to complete the Advent wreath.

**3.** Epiphany is the twelfth or last day of Christmas. It occurs on January 6th, commemorating the day the Wise Men arrived in Bethlehem.

**4.** The Wise Men were Melchior of Arabia, Gaspar of Tharsis, and Balthazar of Saba.

**5.** Melchior brought gold, Gaspar, frankincense, and Balthazar, myrrh.

**6.** Green symbolizes that life continues through the winter and hence the Christian belief in eternal life through Jesus Christ. Red symbolizes the blood Jesus shed at his crucifixion.

**7.** According to legend, in the Netherlands, Belgium, and Luxembourg, St. Nicholas arrives on a boat from Spain on December 5, the eve of his feast day.

**8.** The lyrics of "Silent Night" were written by Austrian priest Joseph Mohr on Christmas Eve, 1818. Franz Grüber, the organist at Mohr's church, composed the music and that same night the carol was sung at Midnight Mass.

**9.** My suggestions are: poem "'Twas the Night Before Christmas", story "A Christmas Carol", ballet *The Nutcracker* and opera *Amahl and the Night Visitors*.

**10.** Edmund Gwenn

**11.** "White Christmas" sung by Bing Crosby, was released as a single in 1942 and has sold 30 million records.

**12.** Boxing Day is the first working day after Christmas. The term probably derives from the European custom of giving Christmas boxes (presents) to tradespeople, servants, and postmen.

# VIII. THE EIGHT DAYS OF HANUKKAH

**1.** d. 1.2
**2.** On the eve of the 25th day of Kislev, the ninth month of the Hebrew calendar, which usually falls in December.
**3.** He was the son of a priest and the leader of the Jews in their struggle for independence from the Syrian Greeks. About 165 B.C. he re-entered Jerusalem and purified and re-dedicated the Jewish Temple which had been defiled by the Syrians.
**4.** After cleaning the temple of Syrian idols, Judah Maccabee and his followers found only one small cruse of oil to light their holy lamps. Miraculously, it lasted eight days. He decreed that ever afterwards Jews would commemorate the miracle by celebrating Hanukkah or the Festival of Lights for eight days.
**5.** It is a special candelabra with eight arms and an extra taller arm to hold the shammash candle. After sunset on each day of Hanukkah, a new candle is lighted using the shammash and moving from right to left. By the last evening eight burning candles stand together.
**6.** b. 44
**7.** all of them.
**8.** It is a top that has four letters printed on it representing the Hebrew message, "A great miracle happened there,". During Hanukkah while the candles are burning, children and adults play a gambling game with the dreidle and a cache of beans or pennies.

# IX. CHRISTMAS FARE

**1.** c Norway; **2.** e Italy; **3.** b Austria; **4.** a Sweden; **5.** d Mexico.

# X. CHRISTMAS CRACKERS

**1.** In Toronto, 1n 1905. Santa Claus arrived by train at Union Station and rode through the downtown streets on a checkered red and black packing case set on a wagon drawn by a team of horses.
**2.** day should be night, and louse should be mouse.
**3.** The ghost of Jacob Marley in *A Christmas Carol* by Charles Dickens.
**4.** On Christmas Day in France, firing stopped in the front line and British and German soldiers met in No Man's Land, the area between the opposing trenches. The soldiers gossiped, exchanged cigarettes, and some of them played football. They met again the next day, but then after some harsh rebukes from headquarters, the firing gradually started again.
**5.** IT CAME UPON THE MIDNIGHT CLEAR

# Mental Health Day Answers

## I. IN THE BEGINNING

1. *Two Solitudes* by Hugh MacLennan (1945)
2. *The Diviners* by Margaret Laurence (1974)
3. *The Handmaid's Tale* by Margaret Atwood (1985)
4. *The Wars* by Timothy Findley (1977)
5. *Obasan* by Joy Kogawa (1981)

## II. LITERARY OFFSPRING

1.d; 2.a; 3.b; 4.e; 5.c.

## III. LIONS AND SHADOWS

1.d,3; 2.c,2; 3.e,1; 4.b,4; 5.a,5

## IV. LIT TRIV

1. Biddulph, north of London, Ontario
2. e. Peter Waterhole Associates.
3. James McIntyre received a kind of renown for his "Ode on the Mammoth Cheese", a tribute to the 7,000 pound giant cheese produced in his home town, Ingersoll, Ontario. The poem first appeared in 1884.
4. Alice Munro won her third award for fiction for *The Progress of Love* and Al Purdy won a second time for poetry for *The Collected Poems of Al Purdy*
5. *A Lover More Condoling* (1968) and *Hunger Trace* (1970)

## V. THROUGH THE PAST DARKLY

1. Frances Brooke's *The History of Emily Montague* (an epistolary love story set in Quebec), published in England in 1769 was the first novel written in Canada by either a man or a woman.
2. Pontiac's Rebellion of 1763.
3. T.C. Haliburton, Nova Scotia jurist, whose character Sam Slick, first made an appearance in 1835.
4. *The Golden Dog* (1877)
5. *The Imperialist* . The setting is Elgin, modelled on Brantford, Duncan's birthplace.

## VI. (MOSTLY) LITERARY KNIGHTS

1. Sir Gilbert Parker (1860-1932)
2. Sir Charles G D. Roberts (1860-1943)
3. Sir Andrew Macphail (1864-1938)

. Sir James MacPherson Le Moine (1825-1912)

. Sir Daniel Wilson (1816-1892)

## VII. SECOND DEBUT

1.d; 2.a; 3.b; 4.c; 5.e.

Note: These titles do not refer to unpublished materials, books written under pseudonyms, or "obscure" works. Brian Moore, for example, published two "suspense novels" with Harlequin in 1951 under a different name. For the record, they were *Wreath for a Redhead* and *The Executioners*.

## VIII. SCRAMBLE

Clue: A Feast of Stephen. Answer: *Arcadian Adventures with the Idle Rich* by Stephen Leacock.

## IX. POOR AND WELL-KNOWN

1. b or c; 2. e; 3. b or c; 4. a; 5. d

## X. WHO AM I?

1. Archibald Lampman
2. Frederick Philip Grove
3. Mordecai Richler
4. Stephen Leacock
5. Al Purdy

## XI. SCRAMBLE (II)

Hugh GARNER, Robertson DAVIES, Marian ENGEL, Rudy WIEBE, and Brian MOORE, all give the third letters R,V,G,E,O which, when unscrambled, spell the last name of Frederick Philip GROVE.

## XII. NAMING NUMBERS AND NUMBERING NAMES

Bliss Carman = 11
"In Flanders Fields" = 16
Northrop Frye = 12

Eleven plus sixteen equals twenty-seven. Twelve goes into twenty-seven twice with a remainder of three. Subtract one from three and you have two or *Two Solitudes* , the Hugh MacLennan novel that won the Governor-General's award for fiction in 1945.